Early Devon Maps

Maps of lands and estates in Devon before 1700

Edited with an Introduction by

Mary R. Ravenhill & Margery M. Rowe

General editor: Dr Todd Gray

Friends of Devon's Archives Occasional Publications Number 1

2000

ISBN 1 85522 728 2

Designed and typeset in New Baskerville 9/10.8 for the Friends
by Mike Dobson, Quince Typesetting, Exeter

Printed and bound in Great Britain by Short Run Press Ltd, Exeter

Inside front cover: Compass rose by Joel Gascoyne
Front cover: Map of Bidlake in Bridestowe, *c*.1609
Left: Compass rose by Joel Gascoyne, *c*.1699
Inside back cover: Compass rose on map of Halberton

Contents

Maps and Commentaries

Acknowledgements

The publication of this volume has been made possible because of grants received from the National Lottery Millennium Festival Awards for All and from the Scouloudi Foundation in association with the Institute of Historical Research, University of London. Both are gratefully acknowledged.

The Friends of Devon's Archives wish to thank the following copyright owners who have permitted their documents to be reproduced in this volume: Lord Petre (nos. 1,5, 17 and 23); Dean and Chapter of Exeter (no.2); the Cary family and Messrs Kitsons, Solicitors (no.3); Messrs Chilcotts, Solicitors (nos. 4 and 16); Exeter City Council (nos. 6, 14, 15, 19 and 20); Robin Langhorne and the Governors of Crediton Church (no.7); Public Record Office (nos. 8 and 12); British Library (no. 9); J.V. Somers Cocks, Esq. (no. 10); Diocese of Exeter (no.11); Dartmouth Town Council (no.18); Dr Katherine Wyndham (no. 21); Messrs Anstey and Probert, Solicitors (for the Pitman family) (no.22); Mrs D.M. Bury (no. 24); Bideford Town Council (no. 25); Mrs and Major Trollope-Bellew (no.26 and the plan of the house).

The small map of Axminster on page 13 is reproduced by kind permission of J.P. Allan and R.J. Silvester and the Editor of *Proceedings of the Devon Archaeological Society* and the view of the ruins at Newenham on page 39 by kind permission of Westcountry Studies Library, Devon Library Services.

The Editors would like to record their thanks to Professor Roger Kain and Dr Todd Gray for their helpful advice and encouragement, to Tony Campbell for providing the Foreword and to Professor Kain, Dr Jonathan Barry and Alan Bacon for supporting the applications for funding. The staffs of the libraries and record offices from which the documents are drawn have been unfailingly helpful; in particular they would like to thank Peter Barber of the British Library, John Draisey of the Devon Record Office, Tim Wormleighton of the North Devon Record Office, Angela Doughty of the Dean and Chapter Archives in Exeter and Adam Green and Sue Berry of the Somerset Record Office. They would like to acknowledge their debt to Mike Sampson, Hon. Secretary of the Friends, for his administrative help in securing the Millennium grant, to Helen Jones for providing the maps on pages vi and 19, to Delphine Jones for designing the attractive cover and to Andrew Teed and Richard Sainsbury for the photography of some less than photogenic maps. Finally, they would like to thank Dr Mike Dobson who typeset the volume and Andrew Gliddon of Short Run Press for their skill and interest in producing such an attractive book.

Abbreviations

BL	British Library
CRO	Cornwall Record Office
DCNQ	Devon and Cornwall Notes and Queries
DRO	Devon Record Office
Ex. D & C	Exeter Dean and Chapter archives
NDRO	North Devon Record Office
PRO	Public Record Office
SRO	Somerset Record Office
TDA	Transactions of the Devonshire Association

Foreword

The manuscript maps that survive from earlier ages have often been valued for their quaintness, for their errors. It can be more rewarding, though, to see them as one of a number of original historical sources, almost invariably incorporating information not found anywhere else. If any modern resident of Bridestowe tries to weave an elaborate hypothesis around the origin of their Hedge Cross they would do well to examine first the 1574 map (No. 4), where it appears rather differently as Edge Cross.

The twenty-six maps sampled in this volume give a good idea of the range of those known from 1550 to 1700. Whatever their appearance, all had a practical, serious purpose. Ownership questions recur, as do rights over land and resources. This particularly applies to Exeter, whose historians are blessed with well-stocked archives. Some of the issues remain topical today, such as rights of way – at a time of 'right to roam' legislation – and access to water, which is likely to become a major concern of this century. Unearthing these original purposes is what gives the documents their historical value and brings them alive. The detective work has been appropriately entrusted to a map historian, Mary Ravenhill, and an archivist, Margery Rowe. Between them they have supplied dates, authorship and the all-important context which lets mute documents speak.

When their work is complete, with the descriptions of well over one thousand maps from the pre-Tithe period (1840), Devon will be one of the few counties to be supplied with a systematic bibliography of manuscript maps featuring places within its bounds, rather than a catalogue of those held accidentally in its archives. Already, some of those in this precursor volume were found (a few, very recently) in repositories outside the county. The identities of the surveyors responsible also underline the way that Devon affairs fitted into the broader national picture, with local figures rubbing shoulders with well-known names like John Norden and Joel Gascoyne.

The visual range of these maps – some stunning, some frankly sketchy – reflects the beginnings of cartographic consciousness in England. What is interesting about the map of parsonage land in Shirwell (No. 11) is that a map was made at all, because such surveys would normally have been textual not graphic. With its wealth of relevant and well-researched information, *Early Devon Maps* will be a worthy initiator of the Friends of Devon's Archives publication series.

Tony Campbell
Map Librarian, British Library
March 2000

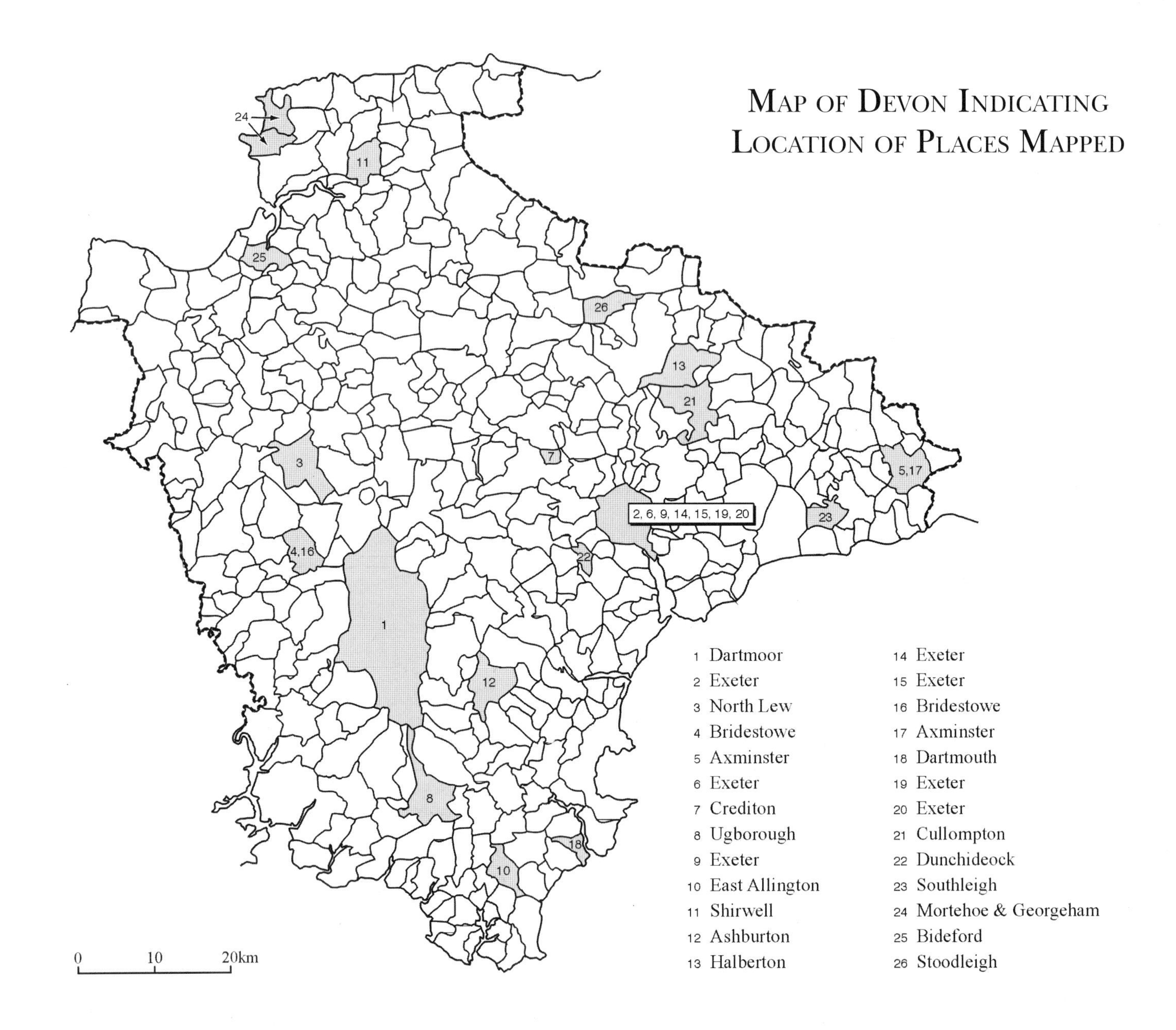
Map of Devon Indicating
Location of Places Mapped
24
11
25
26
13
21
7
3
5,17
2, 6, 9, 14, 15, 19, 20
23
4,16
22
1
12
8
18
10
1 Dartmoor
2 Exeter
3 North Lew
4 Bridestowe
5 Axminster
6 Exeter
7 Crediton
8 Ugborough
9 Exeter
10 East Allington
11 Shirwell
12 Ashburton
13 Halberton
14 Exeter
15 Exeter
16 Bridestowe
17 Axminster
18 Dartmouth
19 Exeter
20 Exeter
21 Cullompton
22 Dunchideock
23 Southleigh
24 Mortehoe & Georgeham
25 Bideford
26 Stoodleigh
0
10
20km

Introduction

Manuscript maps are among the most used documents in local record offices and it seems appropriate that the first volume of Friends of Devon Archives Occasional Publications should feature maps of Devon. It provides an opportunity to make these maps available to a wider public and to bring together documents from several repositories in a single volume. For the local historian large-scale maps can give an insight into aspects of the Devon landscape in earlier centuries, especially when used with supporting documentation such as title deeds and written estate records. A comparison of some of these early maps with modern Ordnance Survey maps provides evidence of the continuity of field patterns. Those researchers with a particular interest in the development of towns will find maps of Dartmouth, Bideford and Crediton (a nineteenth-century copy) included and no less than five maps for the City of Exeter, the latter reflecting the remarkable survival rate of archives for the city from the Tudor and Stuart periods. For the student of cartography, any publication of maps from a county in the South West will be welcomed, for hitherto, Devon has not been the first county that came to mind as noteworthy for the survival of early estate maps. Counties in the south-east of England can produce many more examples. However, recent research has unearthed a good number of manuscript maps for this period which were not known previously and it may be that this would prove to be the case for the other south-western counties.

The 26 maps chosen for this volume have been selected from over 60 maps drawn before 1700 not only because they are visually attractive but also because they are representative of the county as a whole.[1] They are drawn from all parts of the county and illustrate the different reasons for making maps in this period. However, they form only a very small proportion of Devon's manuscript maps currently being studied as part of a larger carto-bibliographical project. This is to list and describe the physical form and content of all the known large-scale manuscript maps of Devon drawn before 1840. It is intended that this more comprehensive work will be published by the Devon and Cornwall Record Society some time after the year 2002. The publication of this smaller volume will serve as a precursor for the larger work and it may alert readers to tell us about the existence of yet more relevant maps which will make the final list more complete.[2] Maps continue to be discovered: one of the maps included in this volume was found very recently by an archivist cataloguing a collection of family papers in the Somerset Record Office. It concerns roads in Stoodleigh and with it was found a house plan, an unusual survival for the first half of the seventeenth century. Both maps will be found at the end of the volume.

To date well over 1,100 maps have been studied in the three Devon record offices, and record offices in five other counties in addition to deposits in the large National Archives and various University and private collections. With such a large corpus of maps to consider it was decided to restrict this initial venture to those made before 1700. We have endeavoured to accompany the illustrations with brief descriptions of the maps themselves together with an explanation of the detail shown and background information pertinent to their making. Some maps have not previously appeared in general cartographic literature; some are the work of surveyors with a national reputation but not known previously to have been active in the South West and yet others are by map-makers new to historians of cartography. What is not new are the reasons why each map was made, for in Devon the problems facing landowners at this period mirrored those elsewhere in the country.[3]

In recent years scholars have added much to our knowledge and understanding of map-makers and their maps. Of particular importance is the recently-published *English Maps; A History* which follows considerable studies by Peter Barber, Sarah Bendall, David Fletcher and Paul Harvey.[4] Peter Barber's contribution to the volume entitled *Monarchs, Ministers and Maps* places early maps in their national context; Sarah Bendall's *Maps, Land and Society* includes valuable introductory chapters for a detailed carto-bibliography of Cambridgeshire estate maps, a theme explored by David Fletcher with reference to the estate maps of Christ Church in his book *The Emergence of Estate Maps: Christ Church, Oxford 1600–1849*. P.D.A. Harvey's many books and articles are essential reading for any study of the period covered by this booklet and *Maps in Tudor England* is of especial importance.

The second half of the sixteenth century saw the arrival of the professional surveyor, a man who was often a peripatetic craftsman working in different areas of the country and in so doing spreading knowledge of new mathematical techniques of surveying. These were expressed in the early textbooks such as those by William Bourne, Ralph Agas, John Norden and Aaron Rathborne.[5] The results were maps and plans which were not only records of the then rural landscape but also often minor works of art in their own right with their decorative cartouches, compass roses and detailed drawings of houses, churches and other buildings. This innovative cartography was increasingly in demand as the sixteenth and seventeenth centuries progressed. The redistribution of land following the dissolution of the monasteries, the improvement of estates and the changing ownership and increasing value of land resulted in the need for the precise identification of property. As far as the maps of Devon were concerned it is interesting to note that although these requirements were, for the most part, met by surveyors from outside the county, there were some local men who attempted to provide the same service. Even so, there were other map-makers who could not attain the standards of the 'professional'. They did not produce precise plans; the principal topographical details were there if not in any correct spatial relationship, but they did assist parties to any legal dispute in understanding the complexities of local geography and did supplement the traditional written surveys.

The maps of Newenham (Axminster) of 1574 and of Shirwell of 1601 are examples where the definition of boundaries was important, while those of Halberton, East Allington, Dartmouth, Stoodleigh and Georgeham were of value in supplementing legal evidence. The map of Kersford, although drawn to identify the areas in the manor held by Henry Bidlake and his tenants, is an early example of a map showing land use. Maps were also made to increase the understanding of problems of land management and improvement as at Wiscombe Park and Grange, East-the-Water, to clarify problems associated with disputes over rights of way as at Ugborough and to show, in a decorative fashion, newly-purchased estates as at Padbrook and Ponsford. A group of five maps of Exeter by John Hooker and Robert Sherwood are of especial interest for they emphasise the care with which the City's Mayor, Bailiffs and Commonalty looked after their property and preserved their rights. This development in urban mapping may be seen in other large towns in the sixteenth and seventeenth centuries but the Exeter City Archives are particularly comprehensive, especially in the survival of supporting documentation.

Our examination of maps has therefore been made with several questions in mind; when and why were they made, who made them and for whom were they made. It is surprising that so many maps are undated and the map-maker's identity not noted, given the amount of work involved in construction and drawing. Of the 26 maps included only nine are actually dated and the map-maker's name is present on only about half of the total. By considering maps in their documentary context it has been possible to improve on this. Most of the maps we have examined are part of the archives of a family, such as the Petres, the Carys, and the Wyndhams, or of a town or city. They were usually accompanied by a written survey and the estate accounts sometimes give the map-maker's name and his payment. Law papers may give clues as to the reason for making the map and provide a date when it was made (as with Sherwood's map of Exeter, 1632–3 and the map of Croyde made for the Incledons at the end of the seventeenth century). In this way we have been able to assign a date for a further 14 cases and provide a possible map-maker's name in four instances. Where maps have been separated from their documentary context at an early date, as with the Public Record Office's Ugborough map which has strayed from its other case papers in Chancery, it is often impossible to provide further information.

One interesting fact to emerge is the contrast between those maps drawn by local map makers and those which were the work of cartographers experienced in more scientific surveying techniques and more sophisticated decorative arts. For example, a comparison of the maps by John Norden, Mark Pierce, Richard Newcourt and Joel Gascoyne, all men with a national reputation, with the maps of Halberton, Wiscombe Park and Georgeham, which were made by local men, serves to emphasise this point. However, the distinction between the quality of the work of local surveyors and that of men with a wider reputation becomes increasingly blurred after 1700 and by the 1740s and 1750s many local map makers could more than hold their own with those from outside the county.

The materials of the maps are worthy of comment. Only eight of the 26 maps in this volume are drawn on parchment. The remainder are on paper. This is surprising given that most deeds of property would have been on parchment at this date. The utility of producing a coloured map seems to have been recognised by the map-maker as no less than 23 of the 26 are coloured. By the seventeenth century certain conventions had emerged concerning the colouring or 'washing' of maps, as the process of applying colour was described. Map-makers were assisted by printed manuals giving advice on the manufacture of pigments and suggestions as to their use[6] although it is difficult to imagine that these books could have been available to local map-makers such as 'Mr Cornish' in North Devon, Samuel Clode and his colleagues at Southleigh in East Devon and Nicholas Townsend in Dartmouth. It is much more likely that their knowledge of the conventional colours used in the maps was acquired from other maps they had seen. Those who drew the Southleigh map certainly seem to have been acquainted with Saxton's map of Devon. The symbols on both maps are similar and Saxton's map had a wide circulation.

Interest begins with the maps themselves but it does not end there. The men who surveyed and translated those surveys into graphic form and the landowners who commissioned the maps are all subjects to be studied. Some of the map-makers, distinguished among their contemporaries, have well-documented lives; others are more obscure. Usually these were local surveyors who were not, at this period, active outside Devon. Some remain little more than mere names such as Tho 'Lo' (Axminster), Nicholas Townsend (Dartmouth) and the Clodes (Southleigh). Barnard Drake (Axminster) and Robert Sherwood (Exeter) are less of an enigma; the former was a sea captain engaged in expeditions to Newfoundland with a little piracy on the side, while the latter was active in the civic life of Exeter. Even John Hooker emerges through these maps as rather more than just the 'creator' of the printed map of Exeter of 1587 which represents his more commonly-recognised claim to fame as a map-maker. Of those whose names were well known amongst their contemporaries only Richard Newcourt came from the West Country. John Norden was known not only for his *Speculum Britanniae* but also as a writer of devotional works, Mark Pierce was active as a map-maker in eastern England and Joel Gascoyne was a chart-maker before becoming a land surveyor for the nobility and the Crown. His work for the nobility included atlases produced for the Robartes and the Grenville families in Cornwall. The patrons in Devon included several West Country landowners such as the Petre family, the Duke of Norfolk, Sir William Courten, the Wyndham family and the City of Exeter, some of whom had acquired their land after the Dissolution of the monasteries.

Local research in Devon has provided new pieces to add to the national cartographic jigsaw of national and local map-makers: it is hoped that other counties in the South West will add to this during the twenty-first century.

Mary Ravenhill, Margery Rowe
New Year's Day, 2000

References

1. This figure includes two maps of which the originals are not now extant. A map of Kingsbridge of 1586 is reproduced in *The Gentleman's Magazine* for 1799 (LXIV, Pt I), 368–69 and a map of Barnstaple, ascribed to 1584, is reproduced in Bruce W. Oliver, 'The Long Bridge of Barnstaple', *Transactions of the Devonshire Association* LXX (1938), facing 194 and in Lois Lamplugh *Barnstaple: Town on the Taw* (Chichester, 1983), 40.
2. List of pre-1650 maps in local record offices, produced on microfiche by the Association of County Archivists, no date. The editors also wish to acknowledge the help given by Dr Todd Gray in drawing their attention to Devon maps held in local record offices outside Devon.
3. Catherine Delano-Smith and Roger J.P. Kain, *English Maps: A History*, (London, British Library, 1999), 112–24.
4. Peter Barber, 'England II: Monarchs, ministers and maps' in *Monarchs, Ministers and Maps; The Emergence of Cartography as a Tool of Government in Early Modern Europe*, David Buisseret ed., (London, 1992), 57–98; A. Sarah Bendall, *Maps, Land and Society* (Cambridge, 1992); David H. Fletcher, *The Emergence of Estate Maps: Christ Church, Oxford 1600–1849* (Oxford, 1995); P.D.A. Harvey, *Maps in Tudor England* (London, 1993).
5. William Bourne, *The Treasure for Travellers* (London, 1578); Ralph Agas, *A Preparative to Platting of Landes and Tenements for Surveigh* (London, 1596); John Norden, *The Surveyors Dialogue* (London, 1607); Aaron Rathborne, *The Surveyor* (London, 1616).
6. See, for example, Henry Peacham, *The Art of Drawing with the Pen and Limning with Water Colours* (London, 1606) and William Folkingham, *Feudigraphia* (London, 1610) among many others. R.D. Harley, *Artists Pigments c. 1600–1835* (London, 1970) discusses this subject in detail.

Further Reading

There is an extensive bibliography on the history of maps and their making in Catherine Delano-Smith and Roger J.P. Kain, *English Maps: A History* (British Library, 1999), 290–312. This includes books and articles published by local record offices on their holdings. P.D.A. Harvey, *Maps in Tudor England* (London, 1993), 117–8 includes a note on 'Further Reading' for maps of the Tudor period.

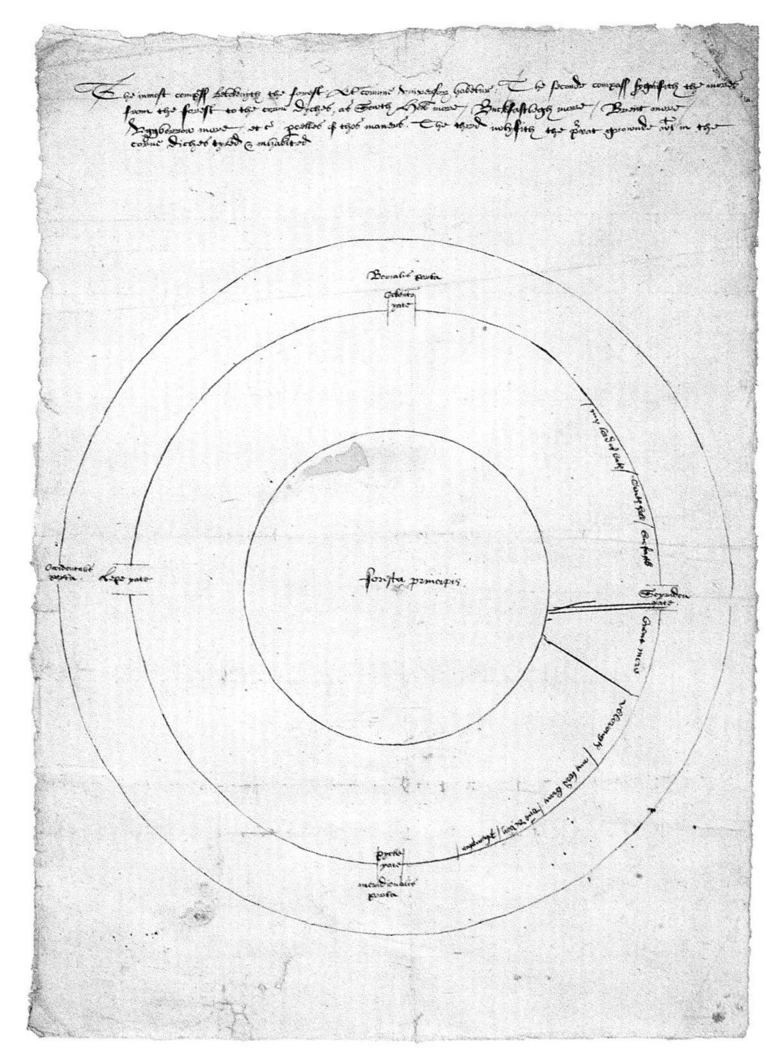

Map 1

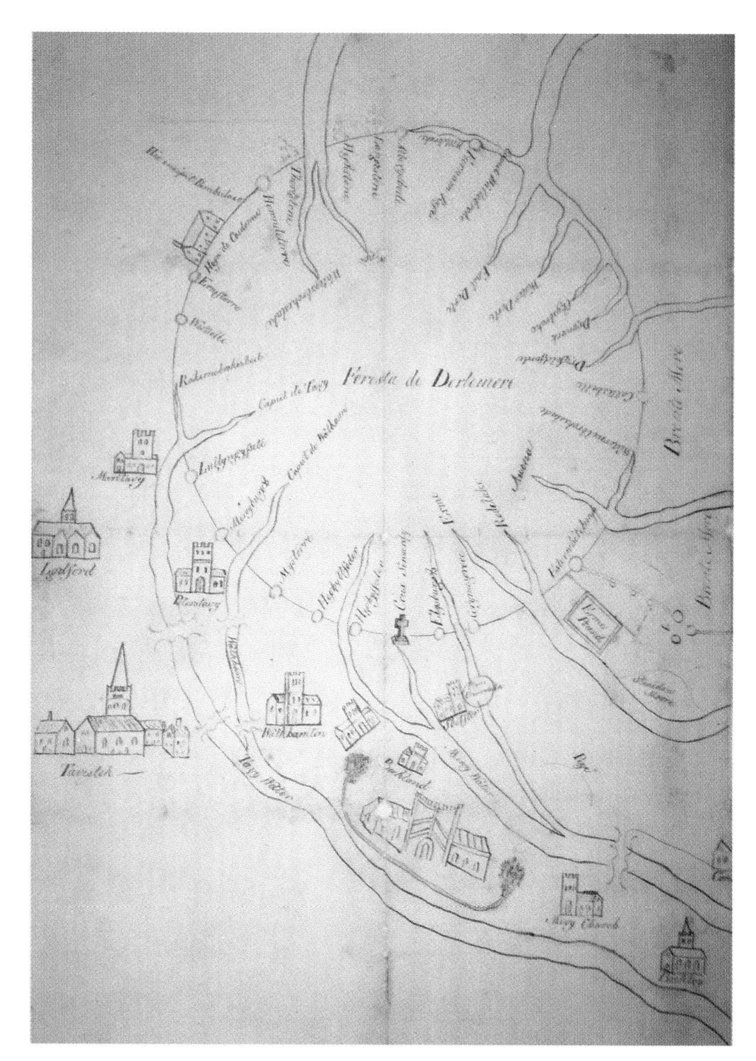

Map 1a

৩ 1 ৫
DARTMOOR

REFERENCE: Lydford Church SX 509847
TITLE: not given
SURVEYOR: not named
SCALE: not given

SIZE: 30.7 cms EW x 42.1 cms NS
MATERIAL: paper, repaired, ink; watermark (hand holding petalled flower)
ORIENTATION: north to top

DESCRIPTION AND COMMENT

This diagrammatic map of Dartmoor consists of three concentric circles with the centre marked '*foresta principis*'. The circles measure 13 cms, 23 cms and 28.6 cms in diameter. In the second circle four gates are marked and named: 'Seyridon yate, Pycke yate, Lepe yate and Ockenton yate'. Areas marked along the edge of the circle are named – 'my lord of bath, South hill, Bucfaste, brent more, Ubborough, my lord bray, *Dns* [Lord] Devon' and 'plympton'. Opposite the gates shown on the third circle are marked '*Occidentalis porta, meridionalis porta, borealis porta*'. East, which should be next to 'Seyridon yate', is not included. The legend at the top reads 'The inmost compass betokenyth the forest *et comm[u]ne universorum habetur* The seconde compass sygnifith the mores from the forest to the corne dyches [fields on the hillside] as south holl Buckfastlegh more Brent more Uggborrow more etc parcelles of thos maners The third notyfith the privat grownde within the corne diches tyled [tilled] & inhabited'.

With the map is an account of the bounds of Dartmoor in so far as they affected the Abbey of Buckfast.[1] It is written in three different hands but appears to postdate a survey of the manors of Buckfastleigh, South Brent and Churchstow dated 1553.[2] The watermark on the map is also consistent with a mid-sixteenth century date.

This was not the first map to depict Dartmoor as circular. A map of about 1500 now in the Devon Record Office has a circle coloured yellow for Dartmoor with streams flowing from it, gates marking rights of way for commoners to reach the moor and churches drawn in elevation.[3] The same format is followed in a map made some forty years later which is in the Public Record Office;[4] it was drawn in response to a Commission of 1542 to the gentlemen of Devon to search and make an enquiry for certain lands in the Forest of Dartmoor thought to belong to the Prince of Wales. John Hooker's *Synopsis Corographicall* of the County of Devon, written *circa* 1600, includes a circular map of Dartmoor but in a slightly different form.[5] At the end of the eighteenth century, the circular pattern was still the preferred way to depict Dartmoor on a map, as may be seen on a map of East Harford and Ugborough produced in a dispute between Humphry Savery and Thomas Lane in 1786.[6] This states that it is based on an 'Antient map', the location of which is unknown. There are also two copies of a map of Dartmoor in the Carew papers in the Devon Record Office which may have been copied from the 1786 map.[7] One of these is reproduced to the left as map 1a.

1. DRO, 123M/E1019.
2. DRO, 123M/E1014.
3. DRO, 3950Z/Z1; for a fuller description see J.V. Somers Cocks, 'Dartmoor Devonshire' in *Local Maps and Plans from Medieval England*, edited by R.A. Skelton and P.D.A. Harvey (Oxford, 1986), 293–302.
4. PRO, Sc 12/2/39. Reproduced in diagrammatic form in S. A. Moore, *A Short History of the Rights of Common upon the Forest of Dartmoor* (1890), 167–8.
5. BL, Harl. MSS 5827, f. 93.
6. DRO, 51/7/7/2.
7. DRO, 2723M/.

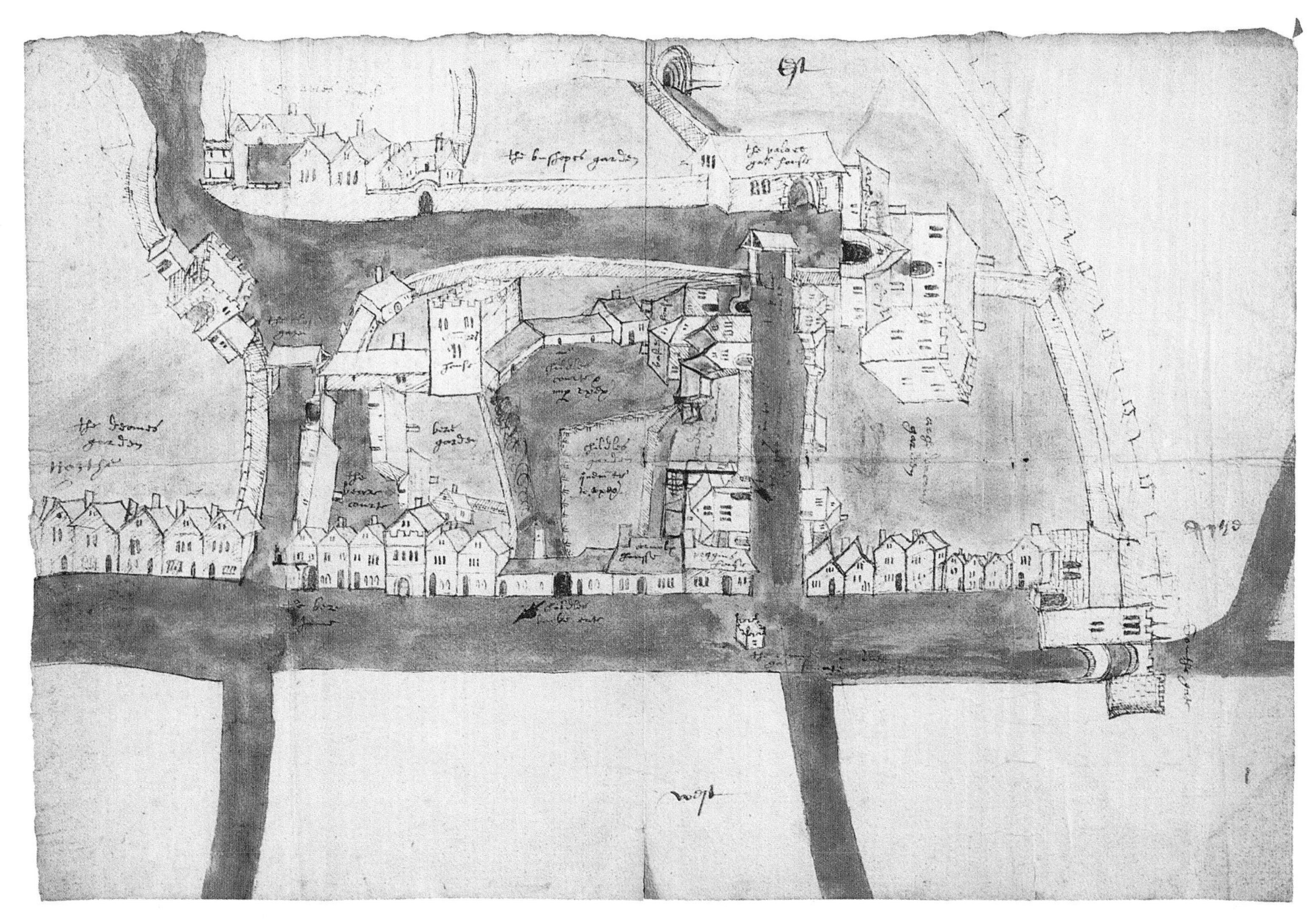

Map 2

between 1553 and 1568

Ex. D & C, M10

ꟿ 2 ꟿ

Exeter, South Street area

REFERENCE: Exeter Cathedral SX 921925
TITLE: not given
SURVEYOR: not named but probably John Hooker
SCALE: not given

SIZE: 27.8 cms EW x 42 cms NS
MATERIAL: paper, coloured
ORIENTATION: east to top, directions spelt out in margins

DESCRIPTION AND COMMENT

The map covers the area from Bear Gate to South Gate, Palace Gate and the bishop's gardens and was evidently produced to give a pictorial representation of houses and gardens to put into context 'a garden at variaunce'. The gardens, including that in dispute, are shaded yellow and the roads are coloured brown. Gates in the Cathedral Close are shown and houses are drawn in elevation with some attempt at reality. In some streets they are shown with opposing horizons.

There is a strong possibility that the map was drawn by John Hooker, the City Chamberlain, who subsequently produced other maps for the City and Cathedral authorities in Exeter. (For details of these maps see number 6 in this volume and the comment on it). Hooker owned property in South Street and probably lived there. He is the only known map-maker resident in the City in the mid-sixteenth century. An endorsement on the map states that John Webbe had received of Matthew Hull on 5 April 1568 some 30 pieces of 'wrytyngs' concerning a parcel of land in Holy Trinity parish whereof 28 are sealed and two are unsealed. The map was presumably in the latter category, the 'sealed' documents being deeds of the property and thus shows that the map was in existence by 1568 at the latest. However, as the conduit in South Street shown on the map was built at the instance of William Smith, mayor, in 1553,[1] it could have been made even earlier, thus pre-dating Hooker's printed map of Exeter by some 20 years.

[1] Richard (and Samuel) Izacke, *Remarkable Antiquities of the City of Exeter* (2nd edition, Exeter, 1724), 127.

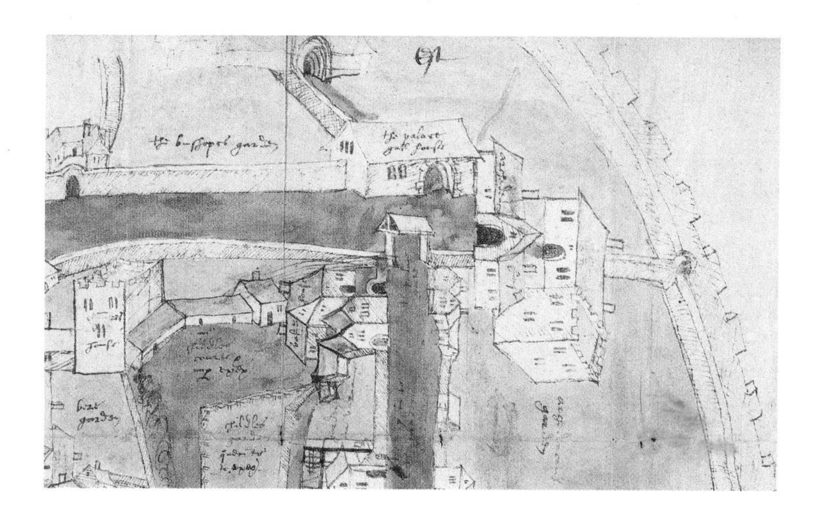

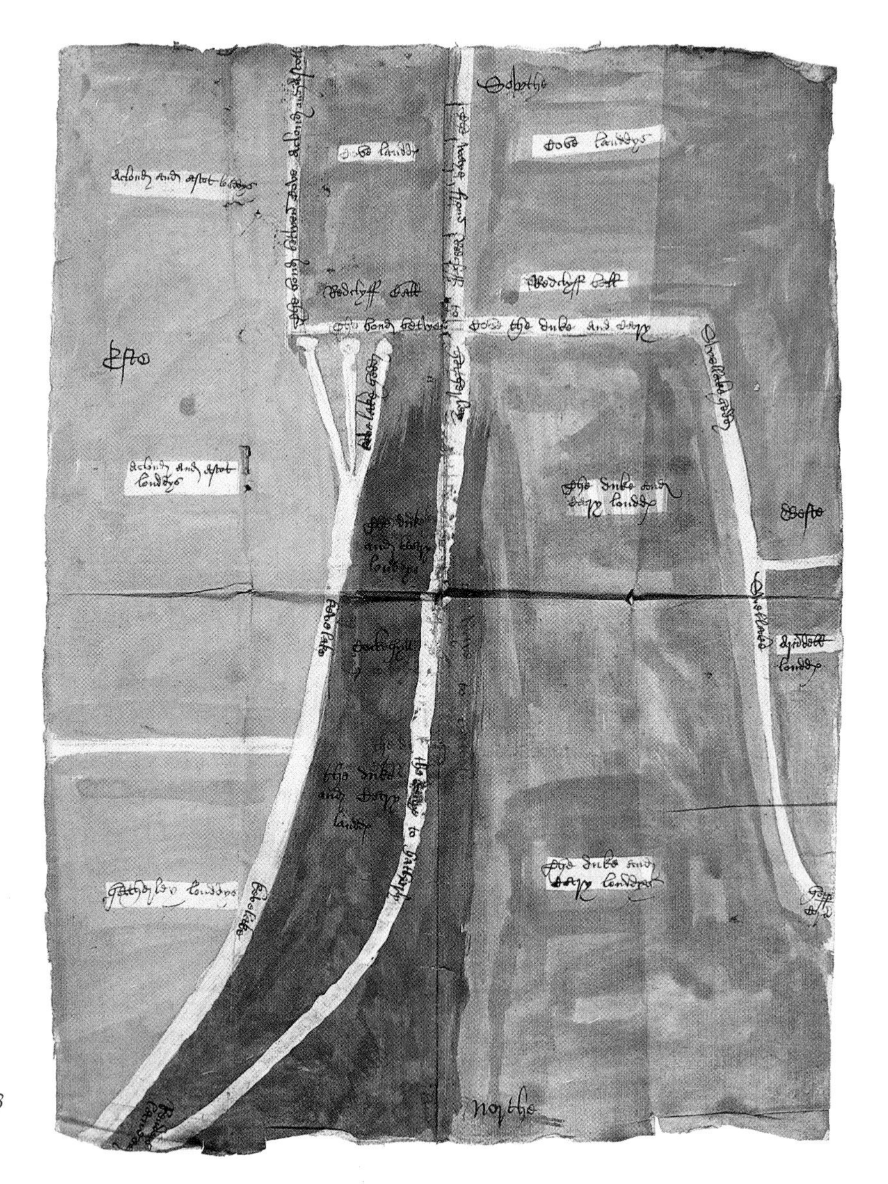

Map 3

DRO, 4088M/Box 7/24

☙ 3 ❧

North Lew, Rutleigh Ball

Reference: Rutleigh Ball SS 510017
Title: not given
Surveyor: not named
Scale: not given

Size: 31.6 cms EW x 42 cms NS
Material: paper, ragged edges, watermark, coloured
Orientation: south to top, directions spelt out in margins

Description and Comment

The map was found recently while listing the Cary papers in the Devon Record Office. It appears to be concerned with the division of lands between various landowners – 'the Duke and Cary londdes', Arundell, Covc, Aclond and Ascott are mentioned. The river Kevelake is shown, rising in three springs and the fields are shown in three shades of green. Some fields are named, including Redclyff ball.

At this stage it is difficult to pinpoint associated documents in the collection which might help to establish a more exact date or confirm the reason for drawing the map. Extracts from court rolls for North Lew for the years 1522–35 mention 'Estredclyffe' and there is a 'View' extant dated 3 April 1549 which establishes boundaries in the parish but does not mention Redclyff specifically: 'The sayngs of Wyllyam Huchyn John Bowdon of Blakeworthy Wylliam Newcomb the older John Northeham the elder of and upon a View takyn for the severall more callyd Holwaye more wyche Bondys extendyth yn maner & forme folowynge that ys to saye from the norther end of Wyllecroft'.

The manors of North Lew and Holloway were granted by the Cary family to Sir William Courtenay on 4 May 1584, which may serve to establish the latest date for the map as no Courtenay lands are shown on it. It is possible that the map accompanied an Agreement between John Arrundell, Lord of the fifth part of the Manor of North Lew, and Thomas Cary, Lord of the other four parts of the manor, concerning the rights of their tenants to graze, till, *etc.*, on the common moor called Westlew Moor. This Agreement is dated 5 September 1563.

'The Duke' referred to appears to be the Duke of Lancaster, owner of the lands in the medieval period.

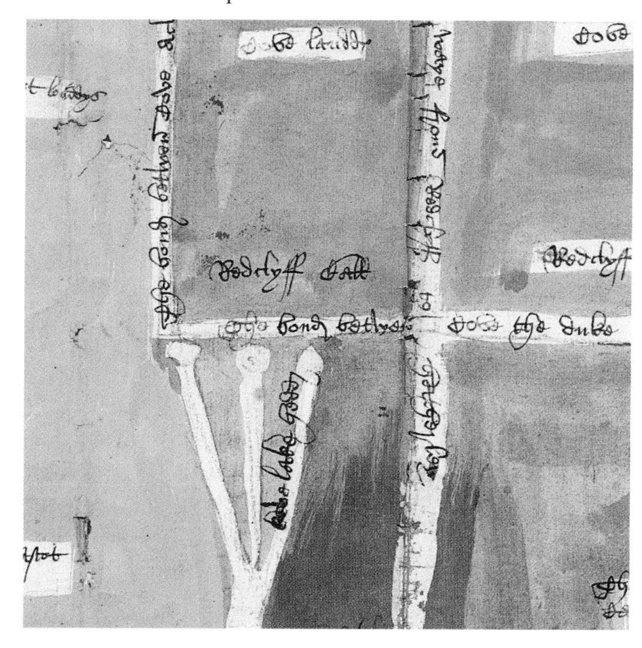

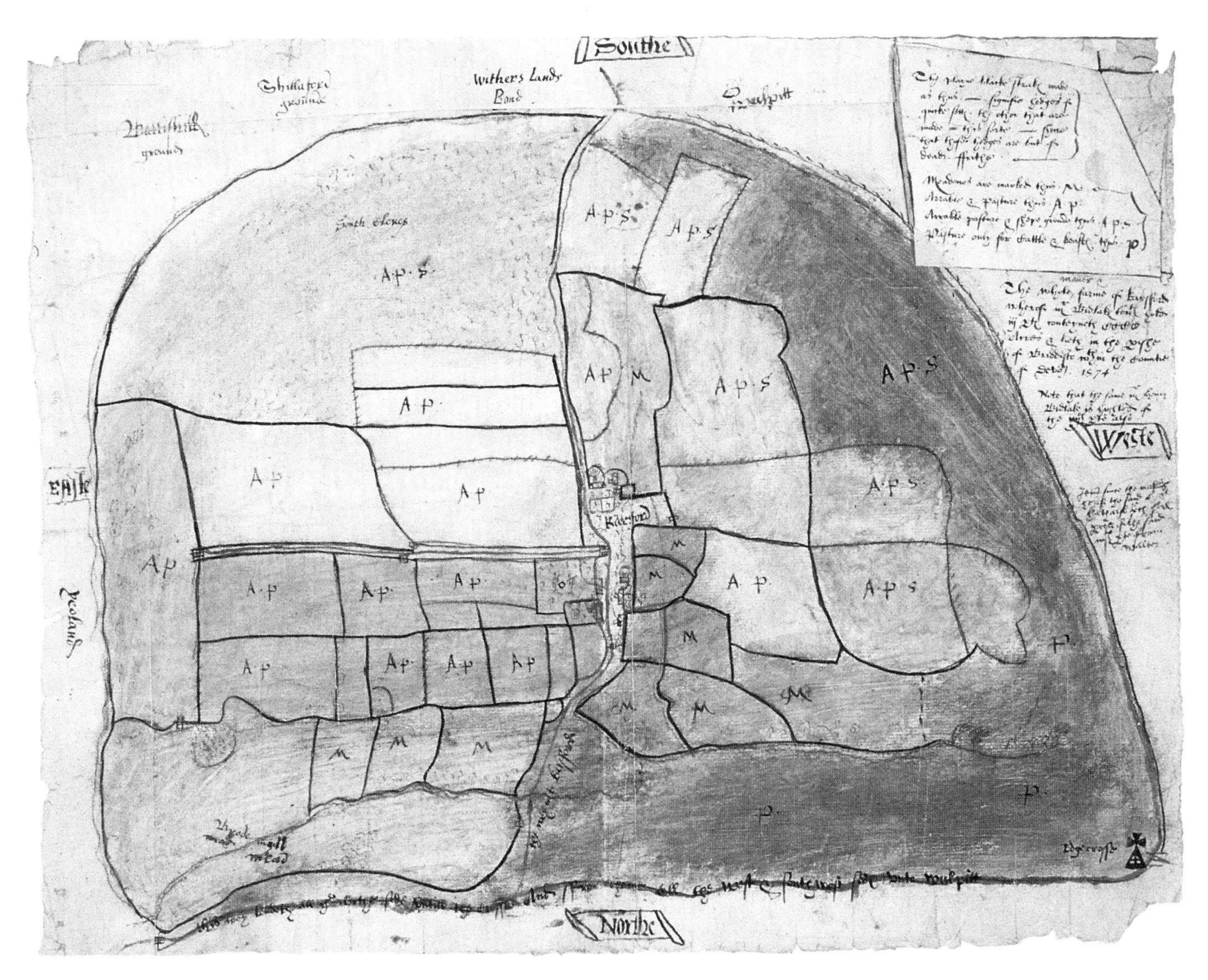

Map 4

ꟹ 4 ꟹ

Bridestowe, Kersford

REFERENCE: SX 499862

TITLE: not given but in the margin the following statement describes the map. 'The whole maner & farme of Karsford whereof Mr Bidlake tenants hold iij partes conteyneth 0000 Acres & lieth in the p[ar]ysh of Briddisto wthin the countie of Devon 1574. Note that the same Mr Henry Bidlake is highlord of the fourth pte also'

SURVEYOR: not named

SCALE: not given

SIZE: 42 cms EW x 33.6 cms NS

MATERIAL: paper, watermark, pot, coloured

ORIENTATION: south to top; directions spelt out on margins

DESCRIPTION AND COMMENT

The farmstead is recorded in the Exeter Domesday Book where it is described as Carsforda. The map is an early example where land use is indicated. Letters distinguish 'Meadowes, Arrable and pasture, Arrable & pasture & shepe gronde and Pasture only for cattle & beasts.' Colour is used to differentiate the various landholdings, not to indicate land use. Hedges of 'quicke settes' and those of 'dead frithe' are marked by different symbols. Other features of interest are the suggestion of reeds and trees along the river banks and the farmhouse drawn in elevation. The cross in the lower right-hand corner is named Edge Cross and it is still present on the modern O.S. 1:10,000 map where it is called Hedge Cross. Red lines, probably distinguishing the three parts of Kersford manor held by Henry Bidlake's tenants, are over-written on the northern boundary. 'This wey bondeth all ye northe side until the crosse ffrom thence all the west and southwest sides on to the wulpit[marl pit]'. A note on the map confirms a Grant dated 1595 which records the purchase of the fourth part of Kersford manor by Henry Bidlake from John Walter and William Walter.[1]

The Bidlake family lived at Bidlake from 1292 until the death in 1792 of Miss Phillippa Bidlake when it passed to the Wollocombes of Stowford.

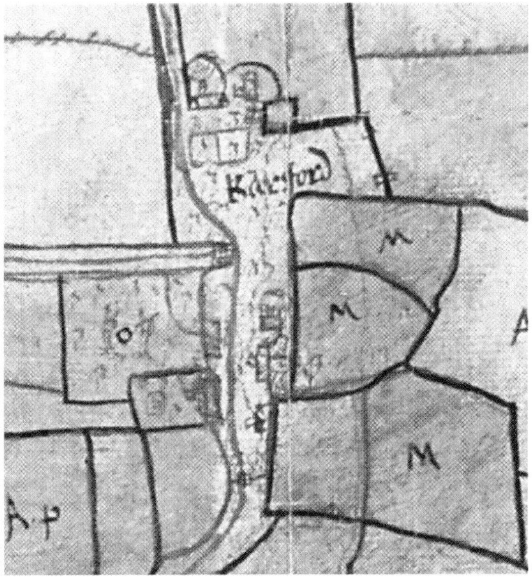

1. DRO, 189M/add3/T3.

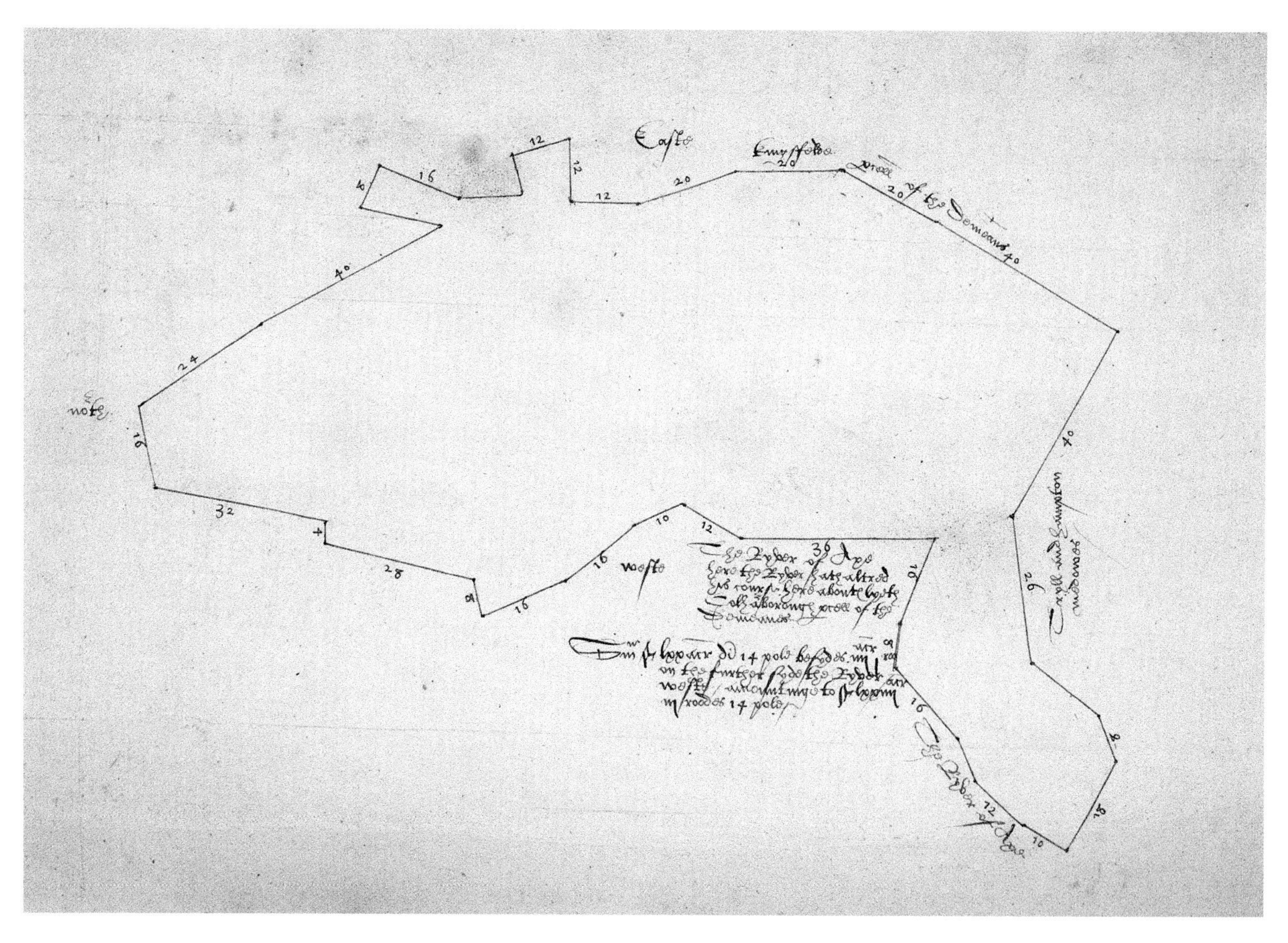

Map 5

ꕥ 5 ꕥ

Axminster, Newenham Abbey lands

Reference: Newenham Abbey SY 287973
Title: (of the volume) 'The possessions of Thomas Late Dewke of Norff' within the countye of Devon'
Surveyors: Barnard Drake esq. and William Buckberte gent.

Scale: not given
Size: 29.1 cms EW x 43.5 cms NS
Material: paper, ink, in bound volume
Orientation: east to top

Description and Comment

This diagrammatic map is one of four such items found in a survey book dated 1574 of the Newenham Abbey lands which were acquired by the Duke of Norfolk after the Dissolution of the monasteries. Although it is only an outline, the orientation is shown, some peripheral estates are named, the land is measured and amounts to over 74 acres. An alteration in the course of the River Axe is also noted. It is essentially a 'working map' and no attempt has been made to make it look attractive, as in the map of Kersford of the same date (see number 4).

Barnard Drake, of Ashe in the parish of Musbury, was born in 1551 and merited a section in John Prince's *Worthies of Devon* (1st edition, 1701) where he is described as 'a gentleman of rare and excellent accomplishments'. He was knighted in January 1585/6 following a trip to Newfoundland with the Queen's Commission where he took many Portuguese ships and brought them back to England as prizes. The seamen from the ships were sent to the prison adjoining the Castle of Exeter and at the subsequent assizes held there, Drake, several of the judges and eleven of the jurors caught a pestilential fever, evidently brought back with the seamen, and died. There is an effigy of Barnard Drake at Musbury church but his burial is recorded in Crediton parish register on 12 April 1586. Like William Buckberte, his co-surveyor, he was a member of the Inner Temple. Drake may have been recompensed for his work on the survey with stone from the demolished monastic buildings which he used to construct Ashe House.[1]

Less is known of William Buckberte but in March 1575 he was granted a lease for ten years by the feoffees (trustees) of the estates of Thomas late Duke of Norfolk of Rudde Meade in Axminster.[2] This was 'in consideration of the painful travail and good service of Buckberte in the survey of the manor of Axmynster and other possessions of the late Duke of Norfolk in Devon'. It is clear that both Drake and Buckberte were responsible for the survey: whether or not they actually drew the maps and wrote the information in the survey book is open to question.

1. J.P. Allan and R.J. Silvester, 'Newenham Abbey Axminster', *Devon Archaeological Society Proceedings*, 39 (1981), 159–71.
2. DRO, 123M/TB557–8.

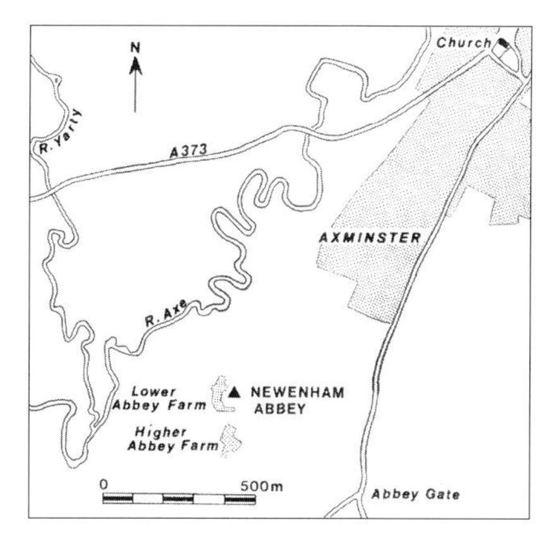

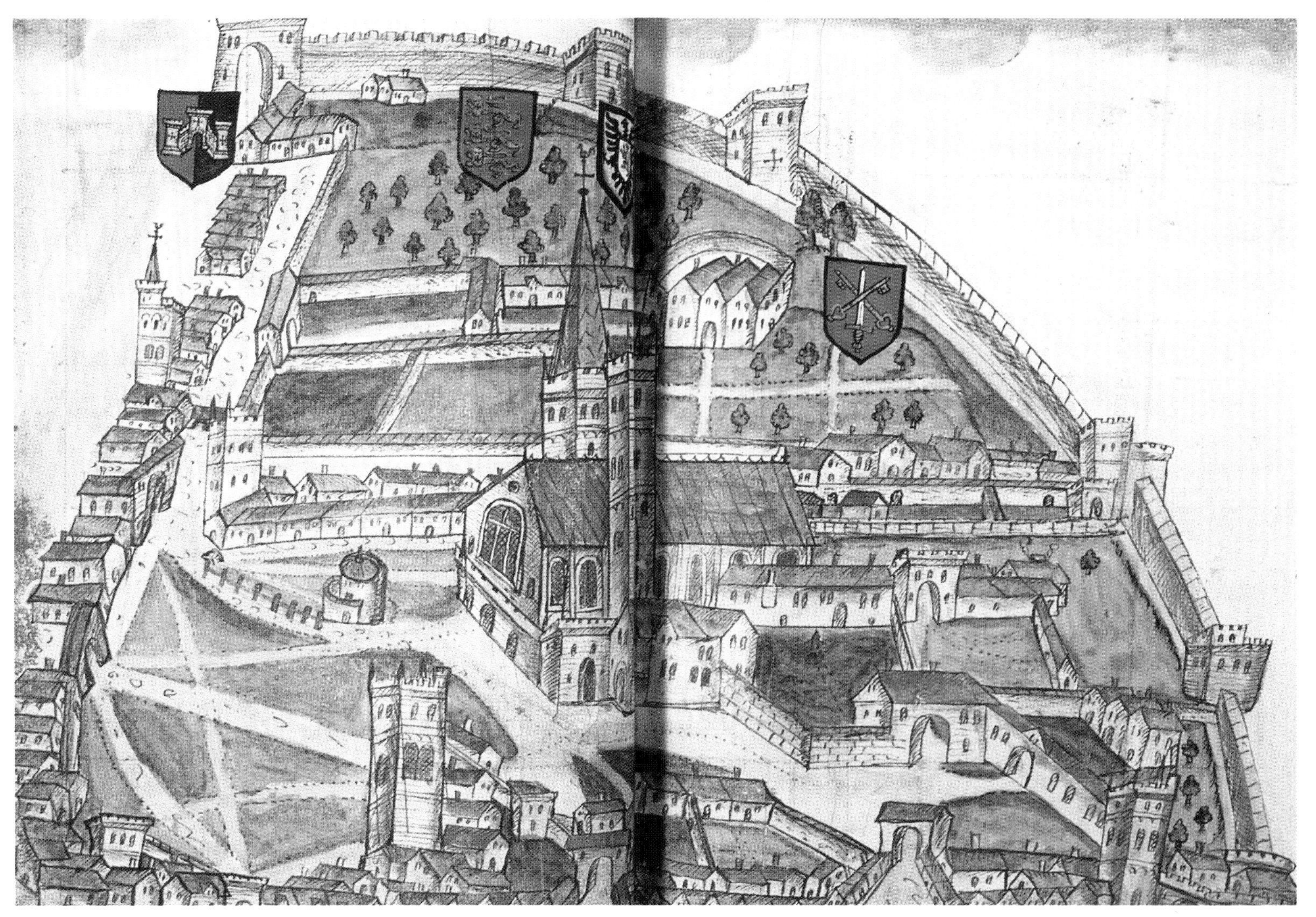

Map 6

ꙮ 6 ꙮ

Exeter

Reference: Exeter Carfax SX 919925
Title: not given
Surveyor: John Hooker
Scale: not given

Size: 34.4 cms EW x 46 cms NS
Material: paper, coloured
Orientation: no direction indicators but East Gate is at the top

Description and Comment

This is one of six manuscript maps of Exeter from the pen of John Hooker, historian and holder of many civic offices in the City. These maps still survive in the archives of the City and of the Dean and Chapter of Exeter, in addition to the well-known printed map of the City which was drawn by Hooker and engraved by Remigius Hogenberg in 1587. The map shown here is bound into Hooker's manuscript history of the City, produced *circa* 1590 and shows the Cathedral and Close, Bedford House, South Street and the City Wall. There are also maps covering a similar area in the City Archives (ECA, Letter 619) and in the Exeter Cathedral Archives (MS 3530) and two other maps covering St Sidwell's Fee, not reproduced in this volume but again with one in each archive. It is supposed that all five items were drawn to show boundaries in the long-standing dispute between the City and Cathedral authorities regarding the ownership and jurisdiction of land in Exeter.

As City Chamberlain, Hooker would have been involved in the drafting of legal deeds which involved 'lymitinge and boundeninge'. Almost certainly he would have seen one particular document concerning a dispute between the Prior of Launceston and some Exeter citizens over lands in St Mary Arches Street. This document would have been passed over with the lands which the City bought after the Reformation. It has a map of the property in dispute drawn by Thomas Harres, public notary, is dated 1499 and has been suggested to be the earliest English document which associates a map with a legal process.[1]

[1] P.D.A. Harvey, *Maps in Tudor England* (The British Library and the Public Record Office, 1993), 103–104.

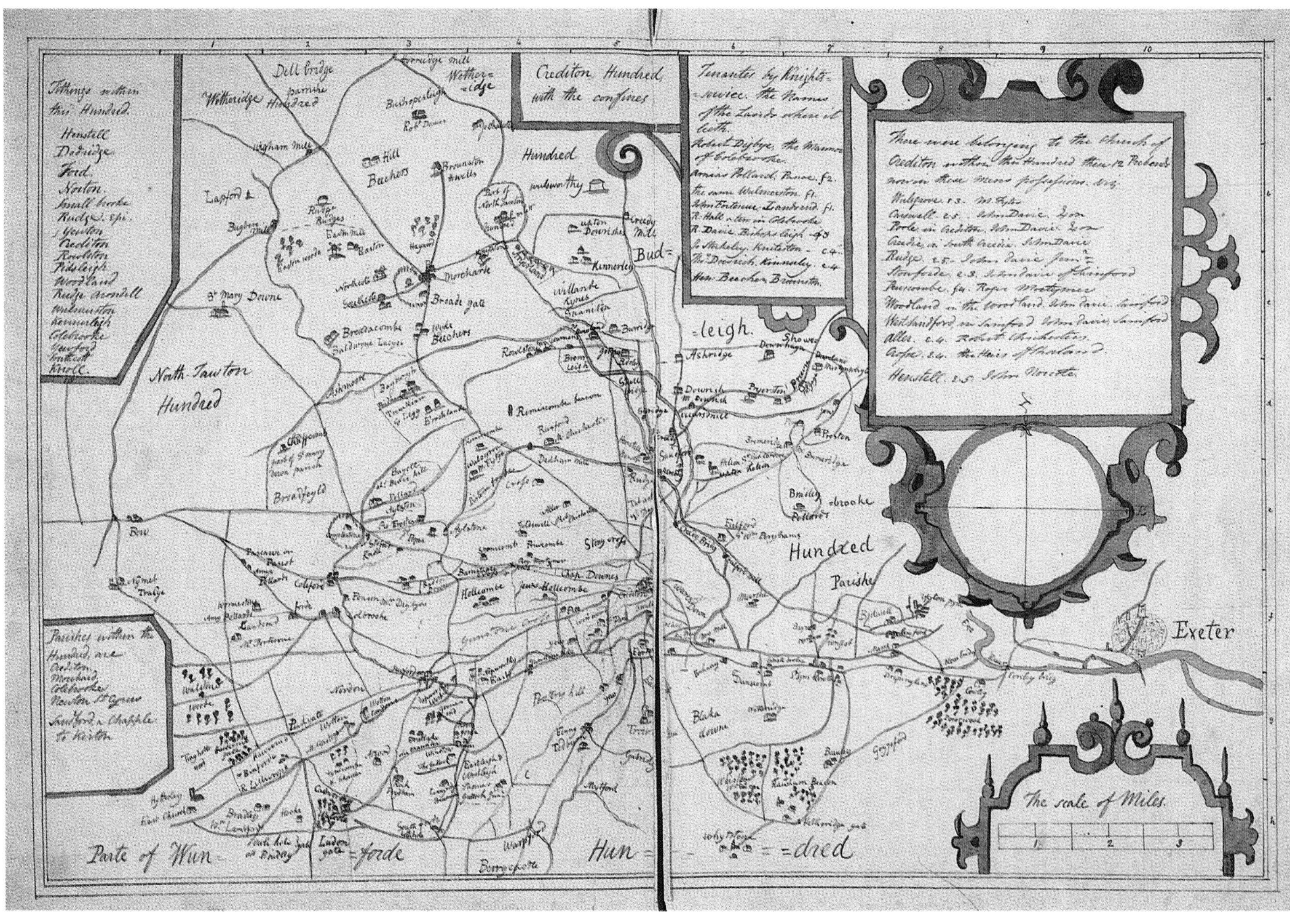
Crediton Hundred, with the confines
Tithinge within this Hundred.
Henstill
Dodridge
Ford
Norton
Crediton
Woodland
Knoll
North-Tawton Hundred
Witheridge Hundred
Dill bridge
Lapford
Bow
Colebrooke
Morcharde
Kinnerleigh
Sandford
Exeter
Hundred
Parishe
Bud-
-leigh
Parishes within the Hundred, are
Crediton
Colebrooke
The scale of Miles
1
2
3
Parte of Wun-
-forde
Hun-
-dred

Map 7

7
Crediton

REFERENCE: Crediton Church SS 836002
TITLE: 'A Terra and perfecte description of the hundred of Crediton alias Kirton in the Countye of Devon made in the yeare of Christe 1598 by John Norden'
SURVEYOR: John Norden
SCALE: 'The scale of perches of 16½ foote'; 1" = 16 perches; 1:3168; 'This Scale Awnswereth all the descriptions in ye Booke The mapp of ye hundred excepted wc hath a peculier Scale.'
SIZE: 60 double-page spreads of maps and text, excluding 2 preliminary pages containing title and scale, bound in a volume 30.5 cms x 39 cms
MATERIAL: paper, coloured
ORIENTATION: direction indicated on each map

DESCRIPTION AND COMMENT

This volume is a nineteenth-century copy of John Norden's maps of 1598. The preliminary title page and the following page showing three scales superimposed on a pair of dividers, together with 25 maps were copied faithfully from the original by the Reverend G.T. Llewellin, Vicar of Sandford. This was fortunate because the original was destroyed in a fire at Creedy Park in 1913. The first page of the volume includes the following:– 'On the 15th May 1595 Queen Elizabeth granted the Manor Burrough and parks of Crediton and her demesne lands of Knowle in the Parish of Crediton in fee socage to be held of the Manor of East Greenwich at the Yearly Rent of £148.8.3½ to William Killigrew and his heirs. Probably the following Survey was made in 1598 for William Killigrew's use'.

The general map illustrated opposite of Crediton Hundred is on a smaller scale than those that follow, but all have features in common; rivers are coloured blue, fields are named and outlined in various colours, trees and hedges are shown by symbols, roads are buff-coloured and buildings are drawn in elevation. The map of Crediton shows the town and its houses in considerable detail.

William Killigrew held estates in Cornwall and most probably came in contact with John Norden when the latter was in that county making his perambulation before producing his *Speculi Britanniae Pars A Topographicall & historical description of Cornwall* for presentation to James I *circa* 1604. Later Norden was engaged in other Surveys for the Crown and Duchy in Cornwall and Devon; most notable were those of 1615–16. These were written surveys of 'Ashburton, Bovie Tracie, Heathfeild, Buckfastleigh, Dunkeswell, Ottery St Mary and Castru Exon' but a small map of the Castle in Exeter was included. This is held in the Corporation of London Record Office. Another more detailed map of the Castle was made in the summer of 1617 when Norden was assisted by his son.[1]

1. BL, Add MS. 6027 ff. 80–81.

See also:

William Ravenhill, *John Norden's Manuscript Maps of Cornwall and its Nine Hundreds* (Exeter, 1974).
William Ravenhill, 'Maps for the Landlord' in *Tales from the Map Room*, Peter Barber and Christopher Board, eds (BBC Books, 1993), 96–7.
Frank Kitchen, 'John Norden (*c*.1547–1625); Estate Surveyor, Topographer, County Mapmaker and Devotional Writer', *Imago Mundi* 49 (1997), 43-61.

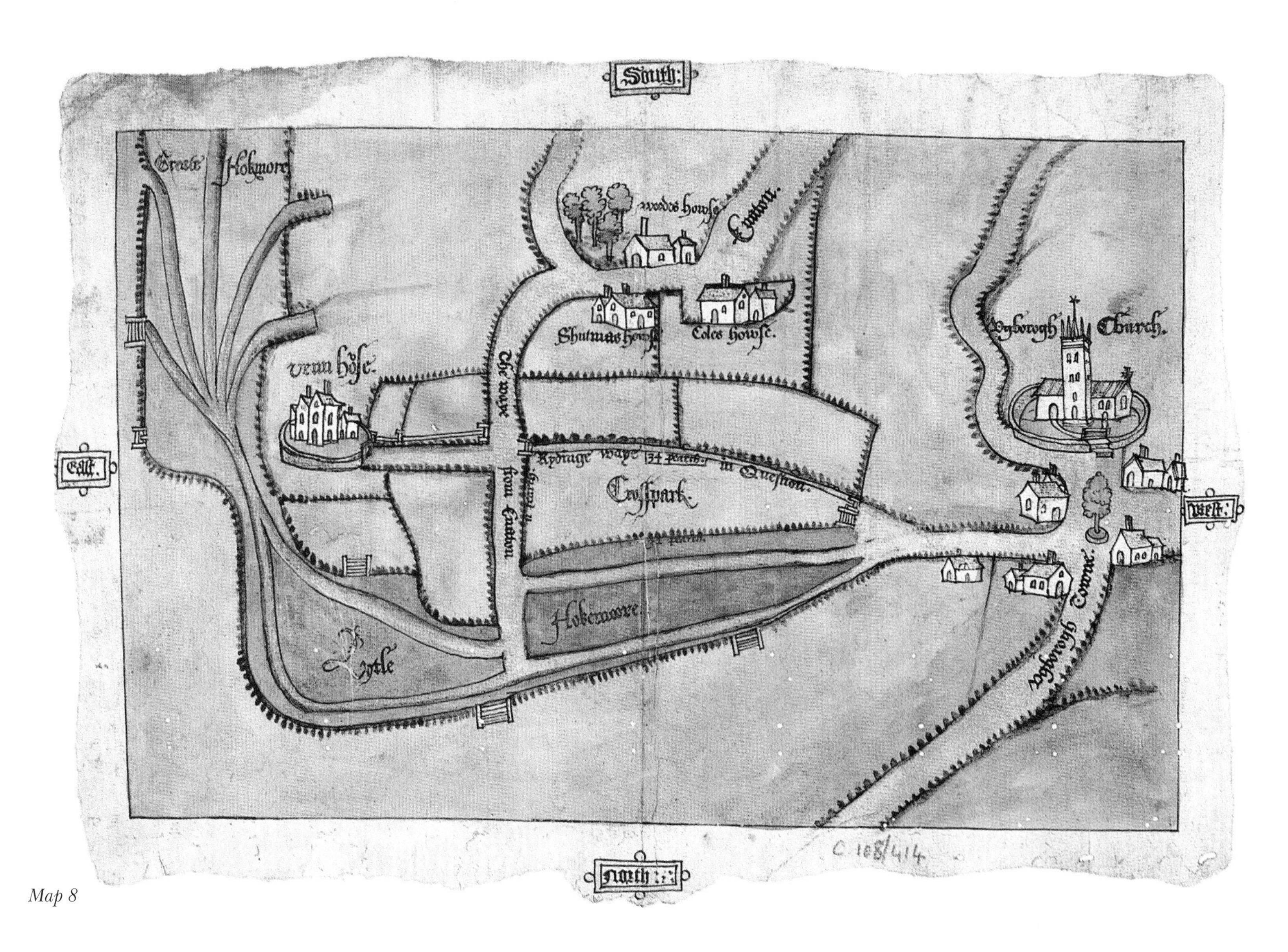
South
East
West
North
Hokmore
Shutmas howse
Coles howse
Church
Rydinge waye
in Question
Crosspark
Hokemore
Lytle
C 108/414

Map 8

꧁ 8 ꧂

Ugborough

REFERENCE: Ugborough Church SX 677557
TITLE: not given
SURVEYOR: not named
SCALE: not given, variable

SIZE: 46.3 cms EW x 31.5 cms NS (as repaired)
MATERIAL: paper, coloured
ORIENTATION: south to top, directions spelt out in margins

DESCRIPTION AND COMMENT

The map shows fields coloured various shades of green, with 'Lyttle Hokmore', 'Great Hokmore' and 'Crosspark' named. Gates and stiles are shown in profile and roads, coloured pink, are marked 'The Waye from Enaton', 'Ugborough Towne' and 'Enaton'. Ugborough Church, Venn House, Woodes House, Shutmas House and Coles House and all other houses are shown in elevation, white with blue roofs. The church is shown on an eminence, possibly the remains of the earthwork.[1] The walls round the church and round Venn House are also of interest.

The 'Rydinge Waye in Question' points to the map being produced in a right of way dispute. Unfortunately, no ancillary papers have been found in the Public Record Office about the case. The class of documents from which the map is drawn consists of Master's exhibits in chancery cases unattributed to any cause, so it is unlikely that the map can now be re-united with other papers, if they exist, to give further information. It is possible that the map is contemporary with the sale of Crosspark by Christopher Savery to Walter Hele in 1586 but there is nothing to substantiate this.[2] Where maps have been taken out of their context at an early date it is often impossible to find the reason for their making and the parties concerned.

There is no scale but there is a statement that the 'Rydinge Waye in Question' amounts to 34 perches. (A perch = 5½ yards). The route is shown as a footpath on the 1:2500 county series 2nd edition Ordnance Survey map of 1906 and is now registered as such on the Definitive Map of Public Rights of Way.

[1] W.G. Hoskins, *Devon* (1954), section on Ugborough.
[2] DRO, Devon Deeds Enrolled, nos. 1254 & 1255, calendared by J.C. Tingey as 'Exeter Castle MSS'.

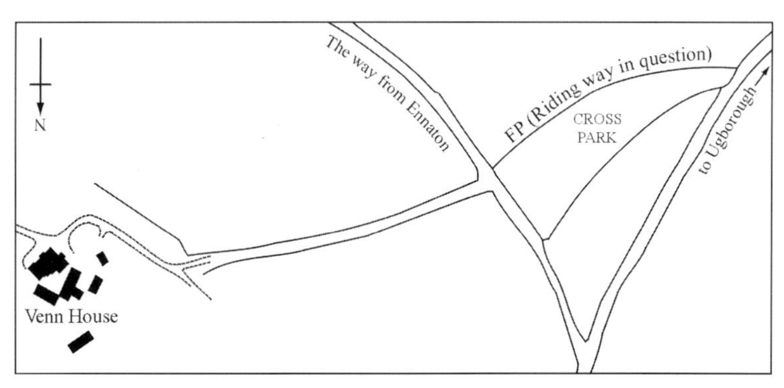

Sketch map based on 1:2500 OS map 1906

Map 9

9

Exeter Castle

REFERENCE: SX 921930
TITLE: not given
SURVEYOR: not named
SCALE: 1" = 30 paces

SIZE: 48.2 cms EW x 48.2 cms NS
MATERIAL: parchment, coloured
ORIENTATION: north to top

DESCRIPTION AND COMMENT

In 1068 the Castle was built on the volcanic knoll now known as Rougemont by William I following his victorious entry into the City of Exeter. The City walls on the north and east formed part of the Castle defences but it is significant that on the south and west William I erected substantial walls and ditches not only as a defence against the the City but also to define the area under his personal control and jurisdiction. This part of Exeter within the City walls remained Royal property and in 1337 became part of the Duchy of Cornwall. It seems that the management of the Duchy Estates was not always as efficient as it should have been and in the early seventeenth century moves were made to increase and maximise Duchy income by recovering lands lost or misappropriated. It was to this end that John Norden made two maps in 1616 and 1617 of the Castle area and these do much to extend our understanding of the map shown opposite.

This map was originally described in the British Museum Catalogue of Additional Manuscripts as 'Temp. Henry VIII' but Peter Barber of the British Library Map Library on the evidence of the handwriting suggests it is more likely to be *circa* 1600. It shows some features which we can still recognise today and others which are more vividly shown on the Norden map of 1617.[1]

The Norman Gatehouse-keep, the original entry to the Castle from the City, and which still dominates the Castle entrance today, is named as 'The Ould Port'. This was blocked up in the later Middle Ages and replaced by that marked as 'ye latter port' which was in existence *circa* 1500. The massive curtain walls remain, though they have been much repaired through the centuries. The north-west corner tower shown partially in plan on the map is more clearly seen in elevation on the Norden map of 1617 but the 'ould' and 'latter' sally ports on the north, although shown on maps of 1617, 1633 and even on a later map of 1756,[2] have long since disappeared. Northernhay Walk, important to the City as a right of way is shown, albeit as a narrow path. It is interesting to note that the map-maker describes the Northernhay Walk as extending from the East Gate to the North Gate whereas by Sherwood's time (see map no. 20) the gate into Northernhay had been moved some distance away from the North Gate. The ditch below the curtain walls on the west, and within the City, had already, *circa* 1600, been made into gardens; they are coloured a different shade of green to distinguish them from the Castle Bank. We know them today as Rougemont Gardens and it is here that the magnitude of William I's defensive works is most striking. The ditch and bank west of the 'ould sally port' on the north remained unfilled as late as the mid-eighteenth century. The Bowling Green was no doubt incorporated into the newly-planted Northernhay in 1612. The 'Cob Batterye' represented a defensive position; the word cob, commonplace in Devon, was used to describe building material of clay or marl mixed with gravel or straw and in 1590 the word Battery meant a platform or fortified work on which artillery is mounted.

1. BL, Add. MS. 6027 ff. 80-81.
2. Exeter Chamber Map Book, ECA Book 58.

See also:
William Ravenhill, 'Maps for the Landlord' in *Tales from the Map Room*, Peter Barber and Christopher Board, eds (BBC Books, 1993), 96–7.

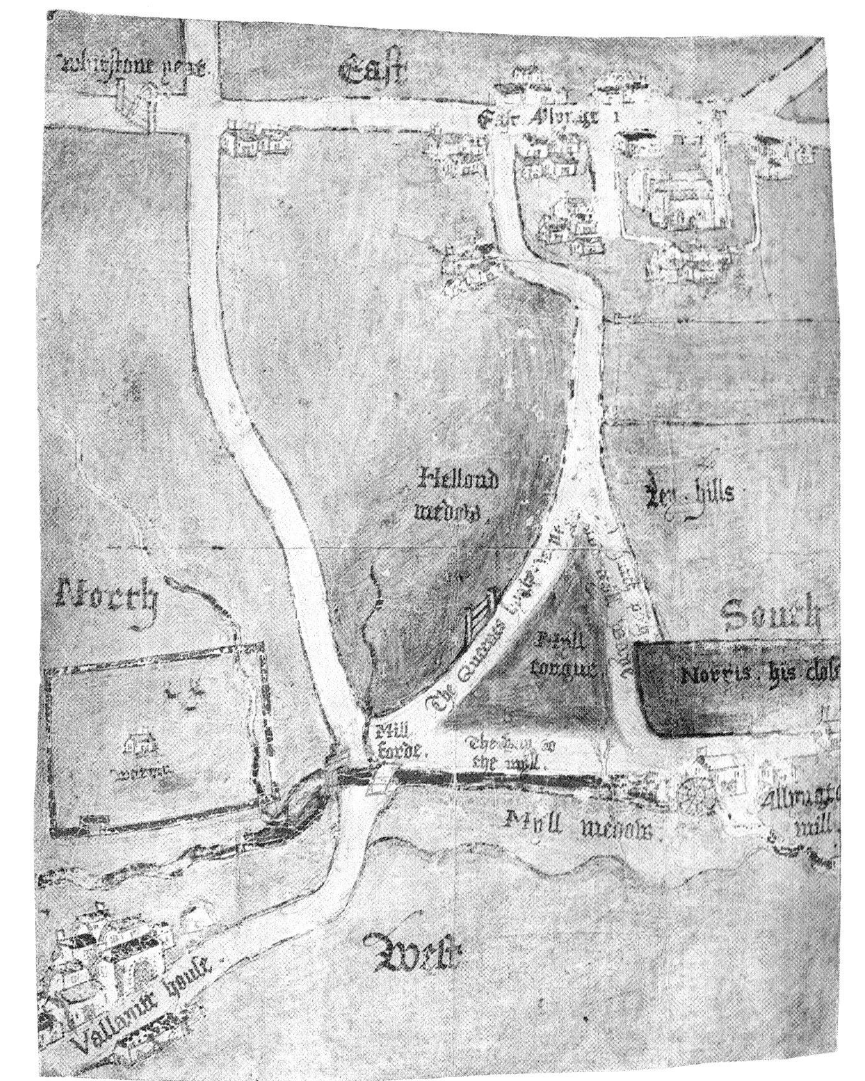

Map 10

℘ 10 ℘

East Allington

REFERENCE: East Allington Church SX 769484
TITLE: not given
SURVEYOR: not named
SCALE: not given

SIZE: 28.5 cms EW x 23 cms NS
MATERIAL: parchment, coloured
ORIENTATION: east to top; directions spelt out on margins

DESCRIPTION AND COMMENT

This map of East Allington in the South Hams is not dated but the road named 'The Queenes hyghwaye' coupled with a lease in the Cornwall Record Office[1] would suggest a date of *circa* 1600 for its making. The lease mentions two grist mills called Allington Mills which with the water supplying them were granted to John Shere the Elder of East Allington, clothier, by Edward Fortescue of 'Vallapitt' (Fallapit). A mill is shown on the south-west of the map with the streams, leats, Mill Forde and a sluice or flood hatch close by. The additional information included on this map is considerable; of particular interest are the detailed elevations of the church, churchyard and cottages in the village; across the road from the village to the north is a gate, 'Whitstone yeat'. This gate may have been intended to exclude from the village, animals grazing the roadside verges. 'Vallapitt House', in the possession of the Fortescue family since the fifteenth century, is drawn in some detail with the enclosure named 'Warren' close by. The usual association of the word warren is with rabbits but originally it was also used to describe a piece of land preserved or enclosed for the breeding of game. The deer drawn here shows the purpose for which this warren was created.

[1] CRO, DD RD 1627.

J.V. Somers Cocks who donated this plan to the Devon Record Office almost twenty years ago described it in more detail in 'Coloured Plan of East Allington *c.*1600', *DCNQ* (Spring, 1981), 261–6.

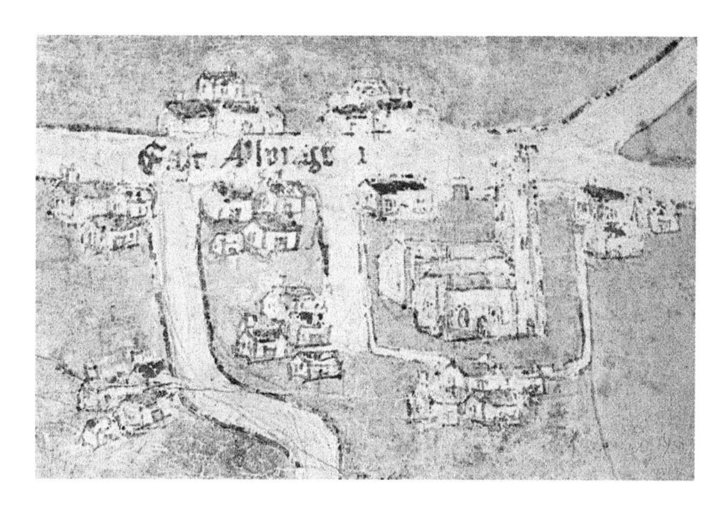

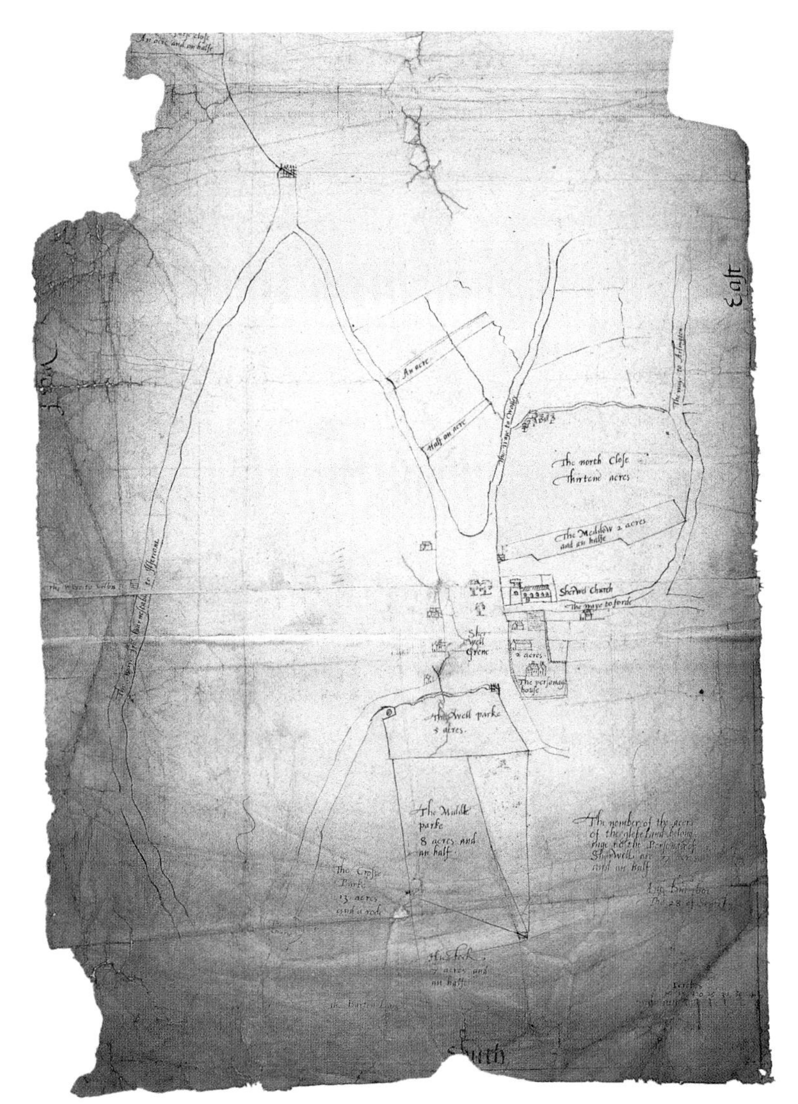

Map 11 – bottom

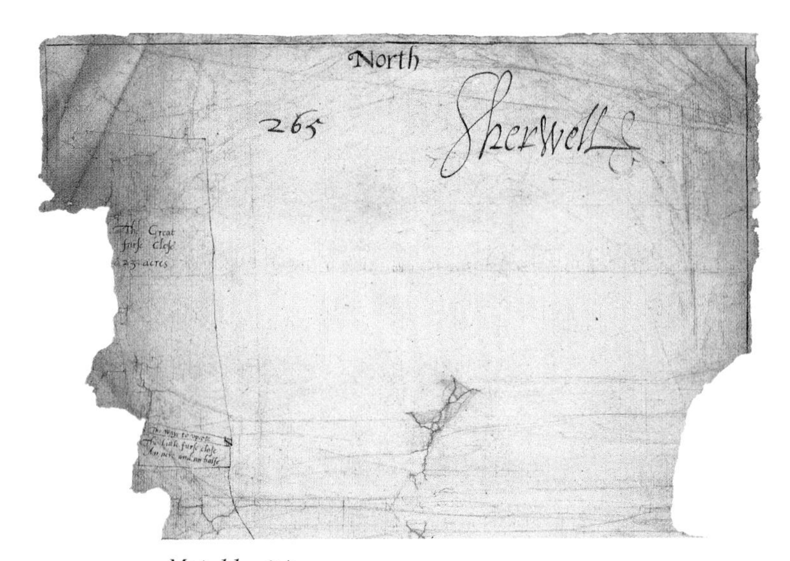

Map 11 – top

➻ 11 ☙

Shirwell

Reference: Shirwell Church SS 598374
Title: 'Sherwell The nomber of the acers of the glebe land belonginge to the Personage of Sherwell are 77 acres and an half Ano Dm 1601' 'The 28 of Septeb'
Surveyor: not named

Scale: 1: 2772
Size: 30.2 cms EW x 59.5 cms NS
Material: paper (damaged), ink
Orientation: north to top, directions spelt out in margins

Description and Comment

Glebe terriers (surveys) were ordered to be made in English dioceses in the sixteenth century to combat the gradual passing of so much church property into lay ownership after the Reformation and to prevent further encroachment. The earliest extant glebe terriers in the Diocese of Exeter are dated 1601. Apart from Shirwell, which is shown here, all are written surveys of the lands which formed part of the glebe and in some cases, lists of furnishings in the parsonage houses. At Shirwell the parish clerk evidently decided to provide a visual representation rather than a written list and so has provided an early map of this north Devon parish. Shirwell Church and the parsonage house are shown in elevation and in some detail and also marked are 'The Quarie'. 'Sherwell Grene' and roads with directions given. A scale bar is provided.

There are written glebe terriers for Shirwell in the Exeter Diocesan records for 1613, 1679 and 1727 but no accompanying maps.

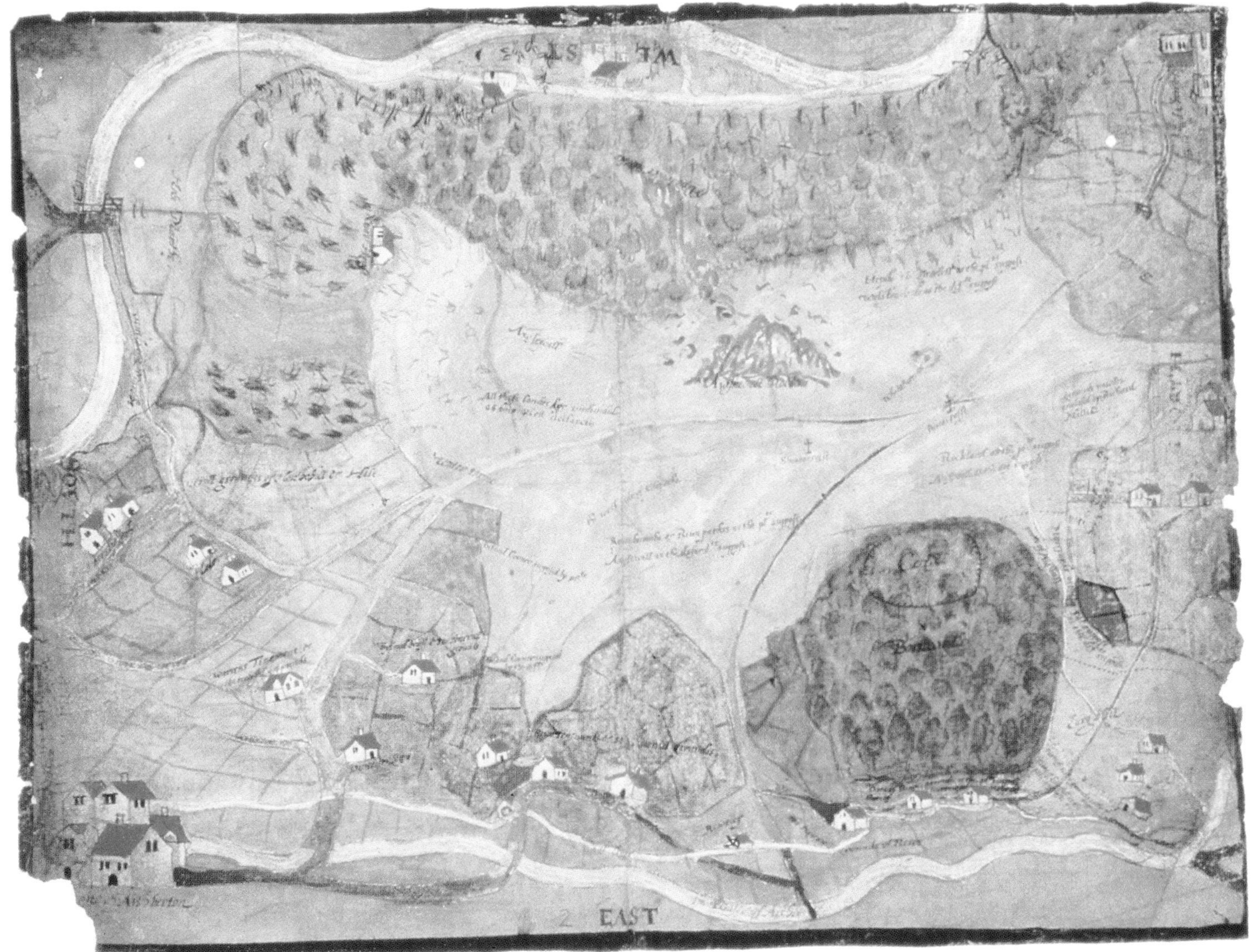

Map 12

1603–1605

PRO, E.134/2 Jas I/H15. Photocopy at DRO, 1057Z/Z1

꧁ 12 ꧂

Ashburton, Auswell

REFERENCE: Auswell Rocks SX 734717
TITLE: not given
SURVEYOR: not named
SCALE: not given

SIZE: 44.5 cms EW x 59.4 cms NS
MATERIAL: paper, coloured
ORIENTATION: west to top, directions spelt out in margins

DESCRIPTION AND COMMENT

The map shows the area to the north-west of Ashburton, stretching from the River Dart on the west to Buckland Common on the north. The town of Ashburton is seen at the bottom left-hand corner and the houses, which are drawn in elevation with red roofs, are intended to be viewed from the east and west sides of the map. Holne Chase, castle and camp are shown, with rocks drawn in profile and an iron mill, probably a smelting house. The map provides our only written authority for the existence of two crosses, 'Shortacrosse' and 'Benecrosse'.[1]

Inclusions such as 'as the defts suppose' confirm the map being drawn for use in a legal case and the written proceedings accompanying the map state that this was between the Attorney General, acting for Richard Miller and others, copyholders of Ashburton Manor, the plaintiffs, against Thomas Forde, William Heywood and Thomas Riche and that the dispute concerned boundaries. The proceedings also recorded that the Commissioners who took the depositions prepared a map to illustrate their evidence and attached it to their report. The Commissioners were Hugh Wyot, Thomas Forde (of Bagtor) and William Wotton and they stated that they had 'repaired to the lands in variance and Survaied and Viewed the same and the Bounds thereof' on 15th January and then prepared the map as well as they could.

Thomas Forde, one of the defendants, was Farmer of the Manor on behalf of the Crown at this date. In 1608, as part of a general drive to increase the revenues from Crown estates, he was prosecuted for alienating Crown lands while a lessee. Outlying portions of the Manor had already been sold off as buyers had become available and these included Auswell (which is named on the map), as early as 1553.[2]

1. *TDA*, 56(1925), 93–4, Appendix A to J.S. Amery's Presidential Address. A re-drawn copy of the map appears on page 94.
2. H.J. Hanham 'A Tangle Untangled: the Lordship of the Manor and Borough of Ashburton', *TDA*, 94(1962), 440–57.

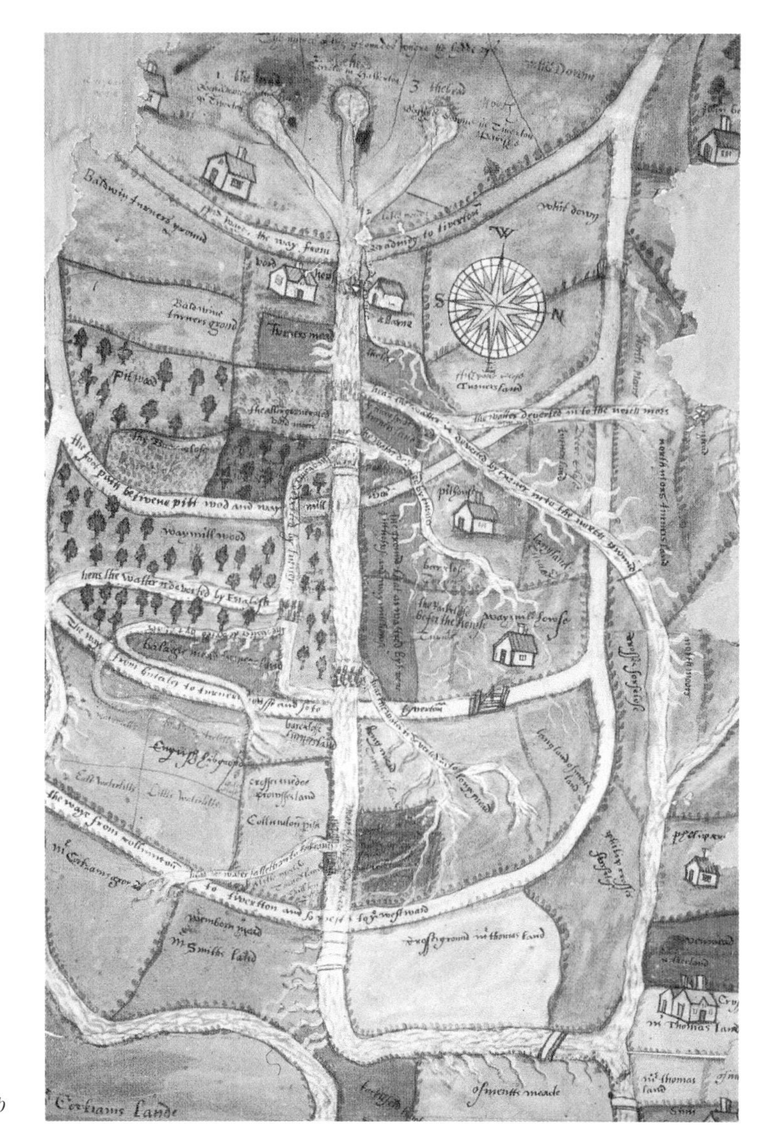
W
S
N
Baldwin furners ground
Pit wood
waymill wood
osmentts meade
m Thomas land

Map 13 – top

13
Halberton

REFERENCE: Waye Mill SS 993090 Moorstone Barton ST 016099
TITLE: not given
SURVEYOR: not named
SCALE: not given

SIZE: 131 cms EW x 43.2 cms NS
MATERIAL: paper, mounted on board, damaged, coloured
ORIENTATION: west to top; 32 point compass rose

DESCRIPTION AND COMMENT

This spectacular map seems to have been made to provide evidence in a legal dispute concerning rights and control over water supply.

The Manor of Moreston had passed to the Wyndham Family on the marriage of Sir John Wyndham to Elizabeth Sydenham in 1575; from 1603 to 1608 there was a Chancery Case between Sir John Wyndham and Abraham Turner concerning the diversion of a watercourse. Depositions in the Somerset Record Office[1] mention such topographical details as the three springs or heads of water, the footpath 'betwene pitt wood and way mill wood' and Ford House which, as well as the name Turner, are all visible on the map. A later record (January 1618) concerns another case, this time between Sir John Wyndham and John Harris – whose name is also on the map – who was accused of 'taking away the earth of a certain bank of the said Sir John Wyndham of the ancient leat part of Moorstone Barton and the close called Camplehays'.[2] Harris lost the case and promised to repair the banks and fill the undermined trench with earth.

The map shows vividly the importance of water, used here for irrigation and controlled by various sluice gates. We are told who has diverted the water and where it is to be used; for example, 'hear the watter is deverted by turner in to the north ground' and even 'hear the watter is rented by John Slad'. The fields and strips are clearly defined and named as are their tenants and owners. It is interesting to note the appearance of such names as Leonard and Manley because Leonard Farm, East and West Manley were settled in 1066, as was Moorstone Barton, and all are still present today. The latter is drawn giving the appearance almost of a fortified manor house; part of an enclosing wall was still visible in 1915 (see below). The roads, one of which is gated, are either named or have their directions indicated. The houses and cottages, drawn in various ways suggestive of their size and importance, for the most part have their owners' names alongside. This map may not have all the features in their correct spatial relationship but the information presented would have enlightened and informed those concerned with the legal dispute.

This map was presented to Exeter City Library in 1934 by Mr Wyndham but the documents relating to it remain in the Somerset Record Office.

1. SRO,DD/WY/Box 22/1.
2. SRO, DD/WY/Box 22/3.

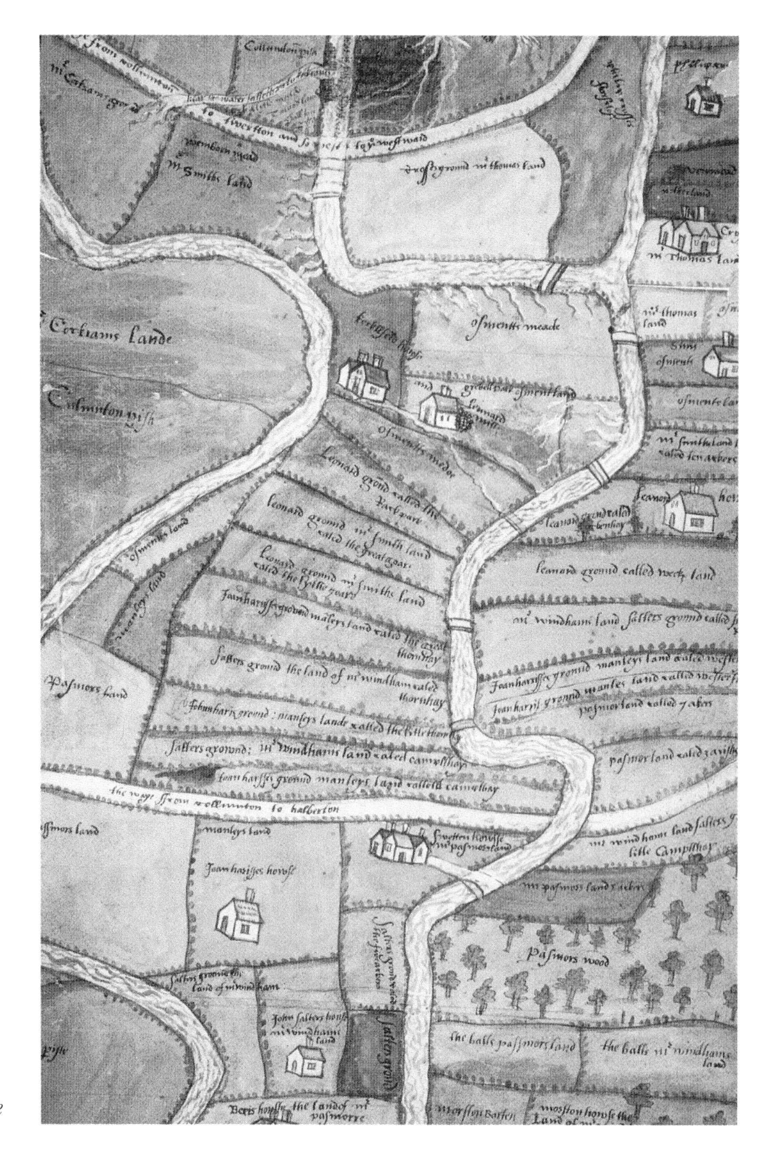

Map 13 – middle

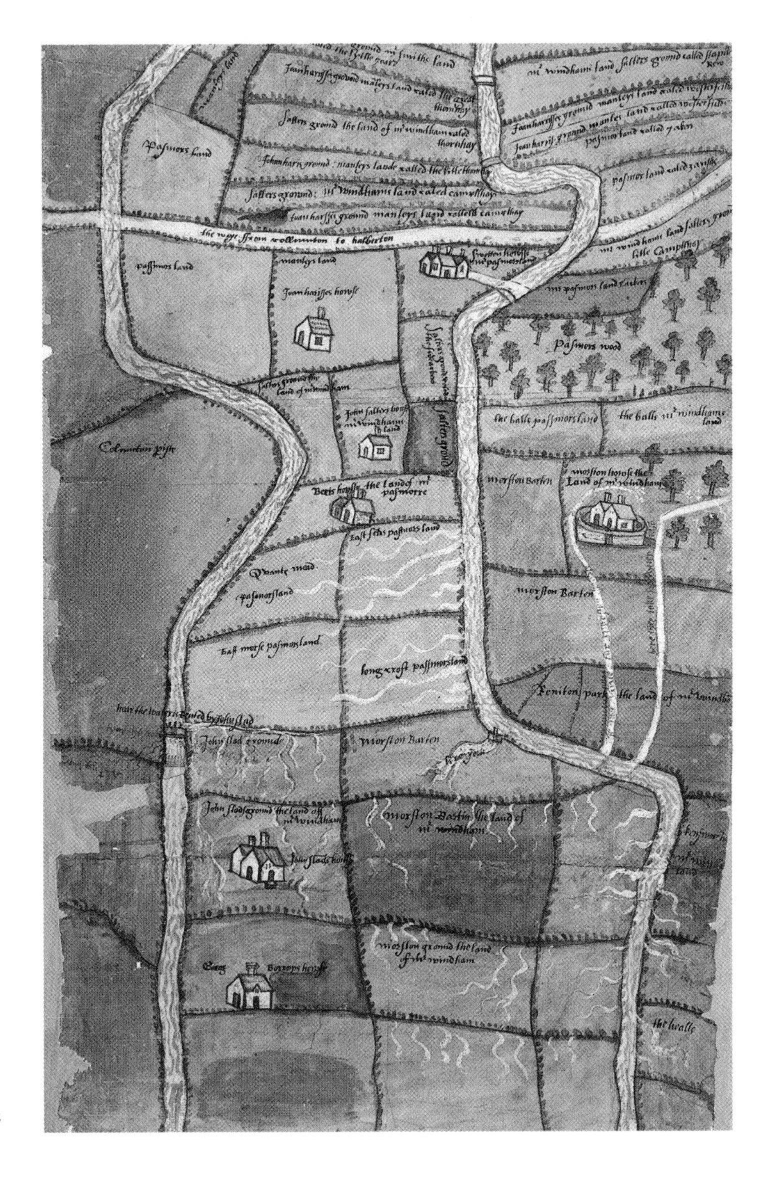

Map 13 – bottom

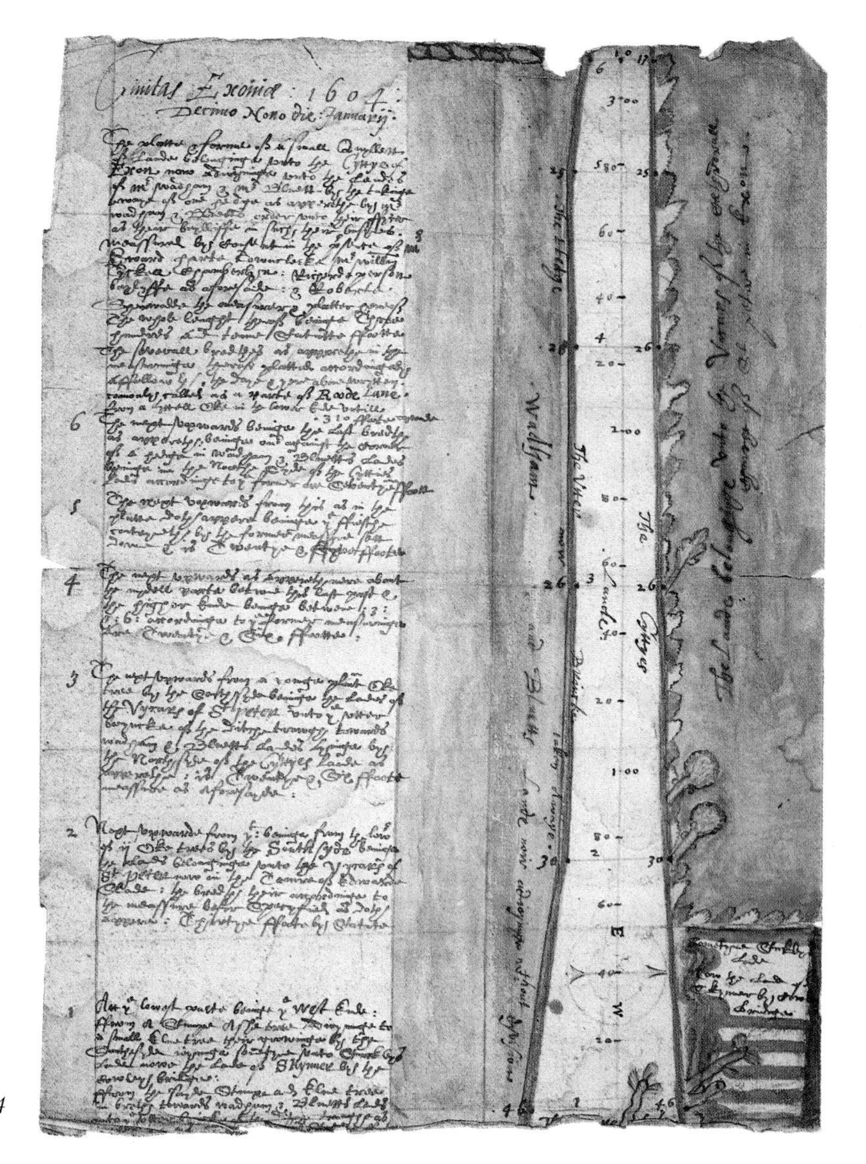

Map 14

14

Exeter, Cowley Bridge area

Reference: Cowley Bridge SX 909953
Title: 'The Plotte and forme of a small Quyllett of Lande belonginge unto the Cyttye of Exon'
Surveyor: Robert Sherwood ('Roberte Sherwodde')

Scale: not given but there are measurements of length and width
Size: 40.5 cms EW x 30.5 cms NS (ragged edges)
Material: paper, coloured
Orientation: east to top

Description and Comment

This is the earliest of the six maps now in the Exeter City Archives drawn by Robert Sherwood. The one shown here is of a small strip of land (a quillet) in the Cowley area. The others are of land on Exe Island and of the whole city (see numbers 15, 17 and 18 in this volume). It may be seen that the map itself, which was drawn by Sherwood, occupies only half the space on the paper. The remainder is taken up with text, presumably in the hand of the Town Clerk or his assistant, describing the occasion of its making and explaining the details shown. It states that Mr Wadham and Mr Bluett, who held land to the north of the City's quillet, had taken away the hedge separating the two landholdings. It was in order to define precisely the boundaries between their land and that of the City that the small strip was measured in the presence of the Town Clerk and the City Chamberlain by the bailiff for Wadham and Bluett and by Robert Sherwood for the City. Details of these measurements are listed precisely, not only as to length (310 ft W to E), but also as to width at clearly defined points, 'From a Stumpe Ashe Tree adioyninge to a small Elme Tree'; 'from a younge planted Oke tree'; 'from the lower of ij [2] Oke trees'. These trees are all drawn individually, coloured in various shades of green and can be used as reference points. To emphasise the 'takinge awaye of one hedge as apperethe by Mr Wadham and Mr Bluets order unto their profytes' the lost hedge is marked by a green line and the 'utter bryncke of the ditche trough' is coloured brown. There is no actual indication of scale but distances are marked at intervals of 20 feet, each being one inch.

Mention of Skynner's land 'by the Cowley Bridge' would suggest that this quillet lay near the present road between Cowley Bridge and Stoke Canon. The map was made to avoid any future encroachment on the City's land as the former fixed visual boundary had been removed.

The surveyor, Robert Sherwood, was born *circa* 1552. There is a record of the admission of a Robert Sherif alias Sherwoode, merchant, to the Freedom of the City of Exeter on 7 November 1580 by fine, although he is also descibed as an apprentice of Richard Bevys. No explanation of the 'alias' can be offered and a John Sherwode was listed as resident in the parish of St John, Exeter, in tax assessments for 1522 and 1524–5. Robert Sherwood married Elizabeth Whetcombe in St Mary Arches church on 8 July 1584 and he is noted as resident in that parish in the subsidy assessments for 1586, 1595 and 1602. His selection as map-maker for the City in 1605 may be connected with the fact that his former Master, Richard Bevys, was mayor in 1603. Sherwood's wife's burial is recorded in St Mary Arches parish register in 1608 but Sherwood lived until 1640 and went on to produce five other maps for the City. The payment of £10 to him by the City Chamber in 1608 may be partly as recompence for the Cowley map and partly as a retainer for future service as City Surveyor.[1]

As may be seen on the section of the map reproduced opposite, the map appears to be dated 19 January 1604 (*1604: Decimo Nono die Januarij*). Until 1752, when the New Style calendar was introduced, the year began on 25 March. Hence the New Style date of this document is 1605 and the modern calendar dating has been used for all the maps in this volume.

1. DRO, ECA, Act Book VI, 336.

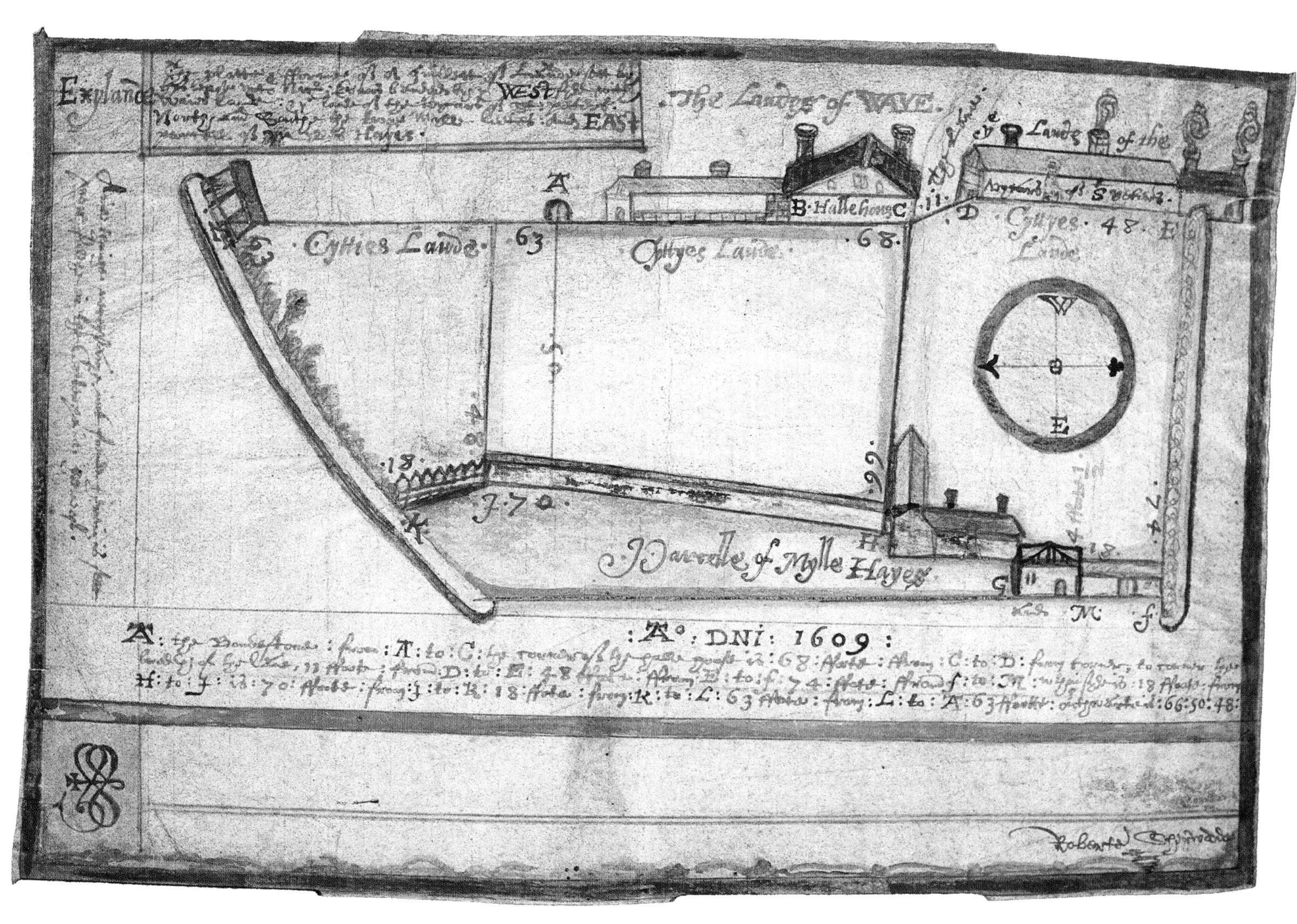

WEST
EAST
The Landes of WAYE
B·Hallehouse C
A
63
68
Cyttes Laude
Cyttyes Laude
Cyttyes 48
Laude
W
E
18
J 70
Parcelle of Mylle Hayes
:Aº DNI: 1609:

Map 15

15

Exeter, Exe Island

Reference: Exe Bridge SX 915921
Title: 'Exylande'
Surveyor: Robert Sherwood ('Sherwodde')
Scale: not given
Size: 24.2 cms EW x 31.4 cms NS
Material: paper, coloured
Orientation: east to top

Description and Comment

This is one of two maps of Exe Island, an area between the west wall of the City and the River Exe, both dated 1609, which were drawn by Robert Sherwood at the behest of the City authorities. They show the 'platte and forme' of land leased to Nicholas Evans, brewer, and describe its boundaries in a panel of text. At first glance the two maps appear identical but Sherwood himself acknowledged that one contains more detail than the other – a note on the side of the map explains that 'Aniething necessarye not founde herein is sett mor fullye in the Conterparte hereof'. The additional information here concerns two roads, one of which is named 'The streete towards the Exe Bridge' and the other 'The Streete towards the Westgatte', thus making a more precise identification of the area concerned.

A second panel lists the distances in feet between various points marked on the map by capital letters, and, lest there be any confusion, figures are also placed between the letters. Thus Sherwood continues the practice of marrying the text and the map seen on the 'quillet' map (see no. 14). Sherwood has signed both maps and illustrated them with his cypher. Each map contains a compass indicator but east and west have been transposed in both maps and this error persists where east and west are mentioned in the description of Nicholas Evans' land.

In 1611 Sherwood received £3. 6s. 8d. from the City authorities 'in full satisfaccion of all his labors paynes taken for the Cittie'.[1] Five years later the City agreed that he should have 20 nobles (a noble = 6s. 8d.) for his fee in attending the City's work and diligent surveying in Duryard Wood, Exe Island and elsewhere for as long as the City wished but specified that he did not have the power to commission any work or to appoint workmen except by order of the mayor and other officers of the City.[2] Even so, he could be described as the first known City Surveyor. In 1621 he received £6. 13s. 4d. for his extraordinary pains taken in the viewing of the City's work over and above his yearly allowance and the City confirmed his payment of £10 per annum.[3] The same source noted that in 1624 (*loc. cit.*, 542) the Councillors were considering a note received from Sherwood asking about payment.

1. DRO, ECA, Act Book VI, 436.
2. DRO, ECA, Act Book VII, 210.
3. DRO, ECA, Act Book VII, 415.

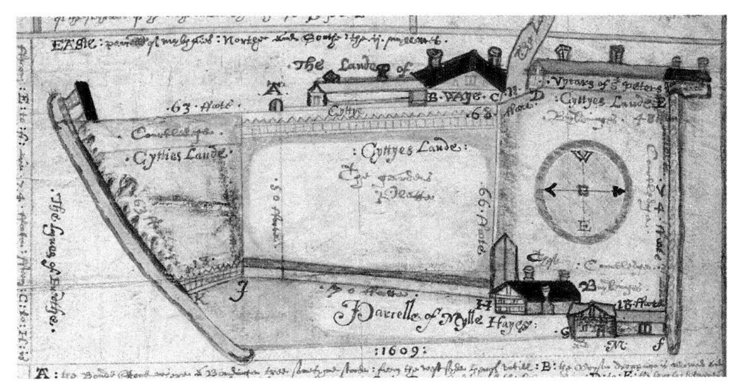

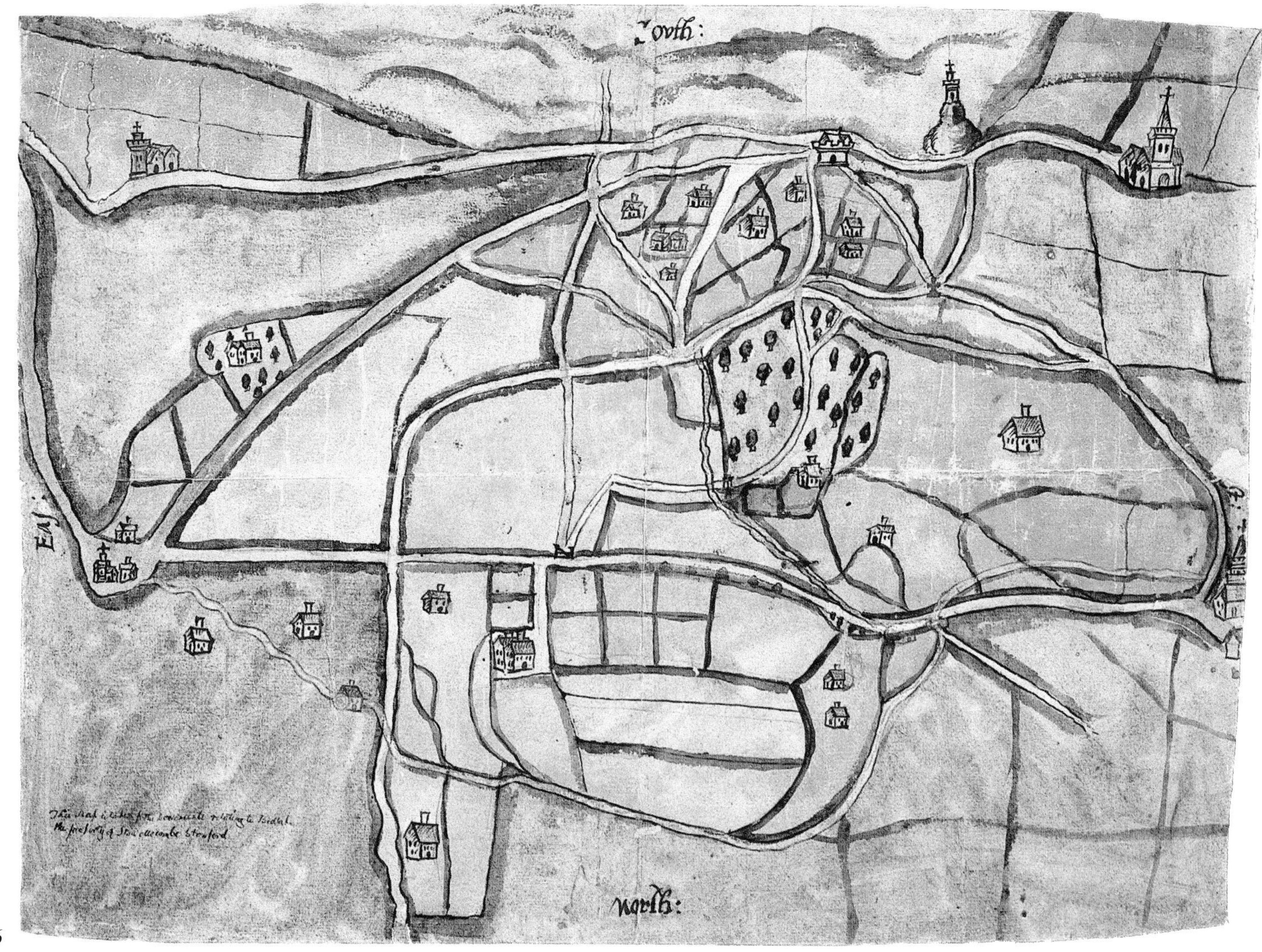

Map 16

ꕥ 16 ꕥ

Bridestowe, Bidlake

Reference: Bidlake House SX 494886
Title: not given
Surveyor: not named
Scale: not given; variable

Size: 55.6 cms EW x 40.6 cms NS
Material; paper, coloured
Orientation: south to top; north, south and east spelt out on margins

Description and Comment

This map was in all probability drawn at the same time as another very similar map in the Bidlake collection.[1] The latter, without colour, but with all the features named, was made to clarify evidence for the defence in a claim made by Paul Ebsworthy against John Bidlake alleging trespass. The action was begun in March 1609 and continued until March 1611. It may well be that the colourful map shown opposite was an elaboration of the legal *aide-memoire* and intended for the personal use of John Bidlake 'to know his own'. In any event it appears unfinished and although not covering as wide an area as the rather crude ink map, the latter does enable us to identify the principal features.

A variable scale is used whereby the centre of the map is on a large scale and away from the centre the scale becomes smaller thus introducing a topological element; this not only concentrates attention on the areas of importance but also introduces information away from them which is essential to an understanding of the position of Bidlake in relation to the wider landscape. This is a practice used on other maps of that period, such as the map of 'Morden Mylles Cuttell'(Cotehele) of mid-sixteenth century date.[2] Thus the Church symbols top and bottom left for Sourton and Bridestowe, the castellated symbol for Lydford Castle, the church symbol for Tavistock and that for Brentor on its improbable but impressive hill, though distant from Bidlake, by their presence enable the reader to orient himself. The abbreviated church symbol, bottom right, reinforces this point. The larger map has a three-tiered castle symbol identified as Launceston; here there is a church which, if not Launceston could be Lifton – in any event both are far removed from Bidlake and so emphasise the variable scale. In the more detailed central area there is much information: Burley Wood, the streams and leats supplying the mills with water, Bidlake House and many other smaller houses. The principal roads and the lanes leading to Dartmoor are shown. Dartmoor is indicated at the top of the map by shading suggesting its rolling hills and undulating relief.

The map has suffered some damage for the marginal indication for west is missing, the symbol lower right is cropped and Bidlake Mill has almost disappeared except for the feint outline of the mill wheel.

The colours used on this map do not follow the conventions which were emerging in the early seventeenth century. Land which is part of the Bidlake estate is coloured a light blue and surrounding holdings brown. The more usual colour for these features was green. The brown tree symbols and the pink used for the roads and lanes were also departures from current practice. For other features the map-maker has adopted those colours in common use.

1. DRO, 189M/add3/E4/1. Audrey Erskine, Brian Harley and Willam Ravenhill, 'A Map of "the way to Deartmoore Forest, the Comen of Devonshire" made *circa* 1609', *DCNQ* 33(1976), 229–36.
2. William Ravenhill, 'The Plottes of Morden Mylles Cuttell (Cotehele)', *DCNQ* 35(1984), 165–74.

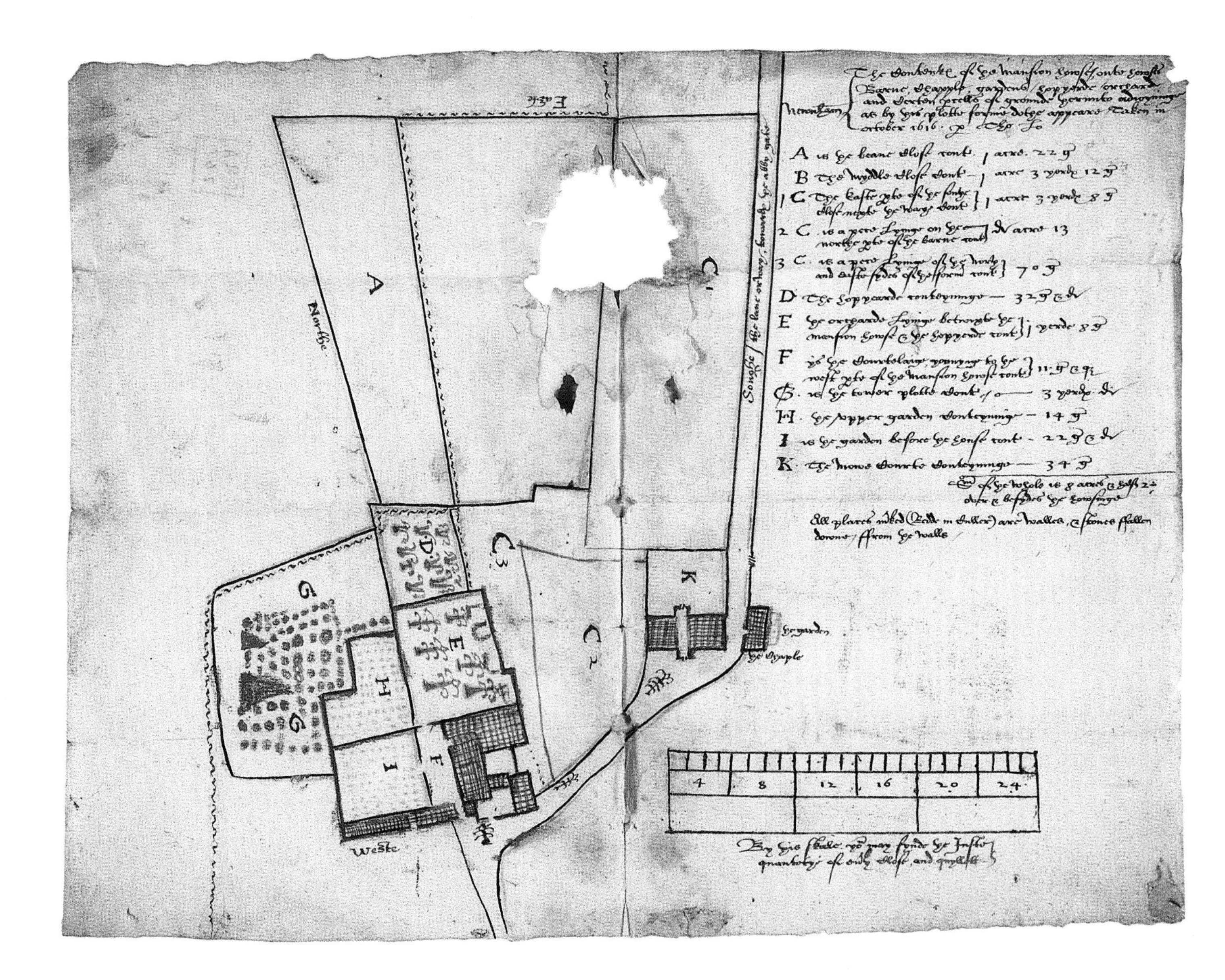

Map 17

17

Axminster, Newenham Abbey lands

REFERENCE: Abbey Gate SY 292971

TITLE: 'The contentes of the mansion house outhouses Barne Chapple gardens hopyarde Orchards and certen parcells of grounde herunto adioyninge as by his plotte forme dothe appeare Taken in october 1616 per Tho Lo' 'Newnham' in margin

SURVEYOR: Tho[mas] Lo

SCALE: triple linear scale but no indication of unit of measurement

SIZE: 30.9 cms EW x 40.2 cms NS

MATERIAL: paper, watermark (pot), slight colour

ORIENTATION: east to top, directions spelt out in margins

DESCRIPTION AND COMMENT

A map of the Newenham Abbey lands dated 1574 is described in number 5 in this volume. Just over 40 years later, in 1616, the lands were mapped again, on this occasion for Lord Petre, who had acquired the lands in 1605 from the Duke of Norfolk.[1] The two maps illustrate the development in technique: the one shown here has a triple linear scale and the surveyor states that 'By this skale you may fynde the Juste quantitys of every Close and quyllett' although he gives no unit of measurement. The map is likely to have been made to support the Petre family's interest in a lawsuit in the Court of Common Pleas concerning the tithes from the demesnes of the Newenham Abbey lands, which were in dispute from 1607 to 1622.[2]

The identity of the surveyor, Thomas Lo, remains a mystery. No other maps in his hand have been traced in Devon, nor has he been found as a map-maker of other Petre properties outside the county. It is possible that he was a local man pressed into service although he seems to have had some map-making skills. There is a [blank] Loring mentioned in the lawsuit about tithes and there is a baptism of a Thomas Loring recorded in Axminster parish register of a likely date, so this person might fill the bill, but it is pure conjecture. It is not unknown for local men to produce quite creditable maps, however. The map of Wiscombe Park in Southleigh (see number 24 in this volume) bears this out.

It is interesting that in 1954 W. G. Hoskins noted that only small traces of the walls remained at Newenham Abbey.[3] By 1616 the walls were already falling down – the map-maker notes 'All places marked Redde in Culler are Walles & stones Fallen downe From the walls'. A lithograph of a view of the walls made by Spreat and published in 1843 is shown below.

1. DRO, 49/26/6/13.
2. DRO, 49/26/10/1–7.
3. W.G. Hoskins, *Devon*, (London, 1954), 325.

Map 18

18

Dartmouth

REFERENCE: St Saviour's Church SX 877513
TITLE: not given
SURVEYOR: Nicholas Townsend
SCALE: not given

SIZE: 38.7 cms EW x 30.7 cms NS
MATERIAL: paper, mounted on board, slight colour
ORIENTATION: north to top; directions spelt out on margins

DESCRIPTION AND COMMENT

This is one of two maps in the Devon Record Office drawn by Nicholas Townsend. He was probably a native of Dartmouth for an entry in the parish registers records his marriage to Jane Heale at Dartmouth Tounstal Church, alias St Clement, on 29 August 1619. An entry in the Dartmouth Corporation Accounts dated August 1620 states that he was paid £1-5s-0d 'for drawing 4 plottes of the towne'.[1] A note on the map shown opposite explains quite clearly why this particular map was drawn. 'This platte was drawn in March 1619 [i.e. 1620] when was had a tryall and virdict against me Jno Roope at the Assizes then held in Exon'. A brief note later in the accounts 'Rd for a sentanc against Mr Roope 5-19-6' records the failure of John Roope's case.

It seems that there was a dispute concerning the maintenance of the way across the fosse. This was a matter of some importance for the fosse formed the dam holding water in the mill pool which allowed the tidal flow to be channelled through the two tide mills. On the second map of Dartmouth of 1620 shading actually suggests this tidal flow.[2]

There is also much information about early seventeenth century Dartmouth on this map. Houses in the two riverside settlements of Hardness in the north and Clifton on the south are drawn in elevation facing each other across the streets, two of which are gated. The New Quay which had been constructed some time after 1574, is shown in colour with more houses along the new waterfront. St Saviour's church, tree symbols, wells and boundary stones add to the picture of Dartmouth in 1620.

Hawley Hall, one of the few buildings to be named, is significant for it commemorates more than the name of John Hawley. He is remembered as the greatest of all the merchants and shipmasters of his day (late fourteenth century) and it is probable that, following Chaucer's visit in 1373, he was immortalised as the Shipman in the *Canterbury Tales*, although not perhaps in terms that he or Dartmouth would have welcomed. Dartmouth declined after Hawley's death in 1408 but his name obviously was not forgotten in the town.

The early seventeenth century saw a return of Dartmouth's commercial prosperity with the revival of the cloth trade and the development of the Newfoundland fishing trade, but this map, because it was concerned with a legal dispute only, does not give any immediate impression of a town engaged in busy and varied maritime activities. However, that picture is vividly conveyed in Townsend's other map of 1620 where ocean-going and smaller vessels are shown in the river and tied up at the quays, with a crane on the quay close to the church ready to load and unload cargo. The variety of information included on two maps of the same area constructed at the same time illustrates the need for care in the interpretation of the evidence they provide. After all, Nicholas Townsend was paid for four 'plottes of the towne'; it is intriguing to speculate what would have been the demands of the Dartmouth Corporation when they were commissioned. In no case would any one map have represented, or been intended to represent, a complete picture of Dartmouth in the second decade of the seventeenth century.

1. DRO, DD 61964.
2. DRO, R9/1/Z/33.

See also:
Todd Gray, 'Fishing and the Commercial World of Early Stuart Dartmouth', in *Tudor and Stuart Devon*, Todd Gray *et al.* eds (Exeter, 1992), 173–99.
P. Russell, *Dartmouth* (London, 1950).
R. Freeman, *Dartmouth* (Dartmouth, 1983), also references to John Hawley and John Roope in *The New Maritime History of Devon I*, Michael Duffy *et al.* eds (London, 1992).

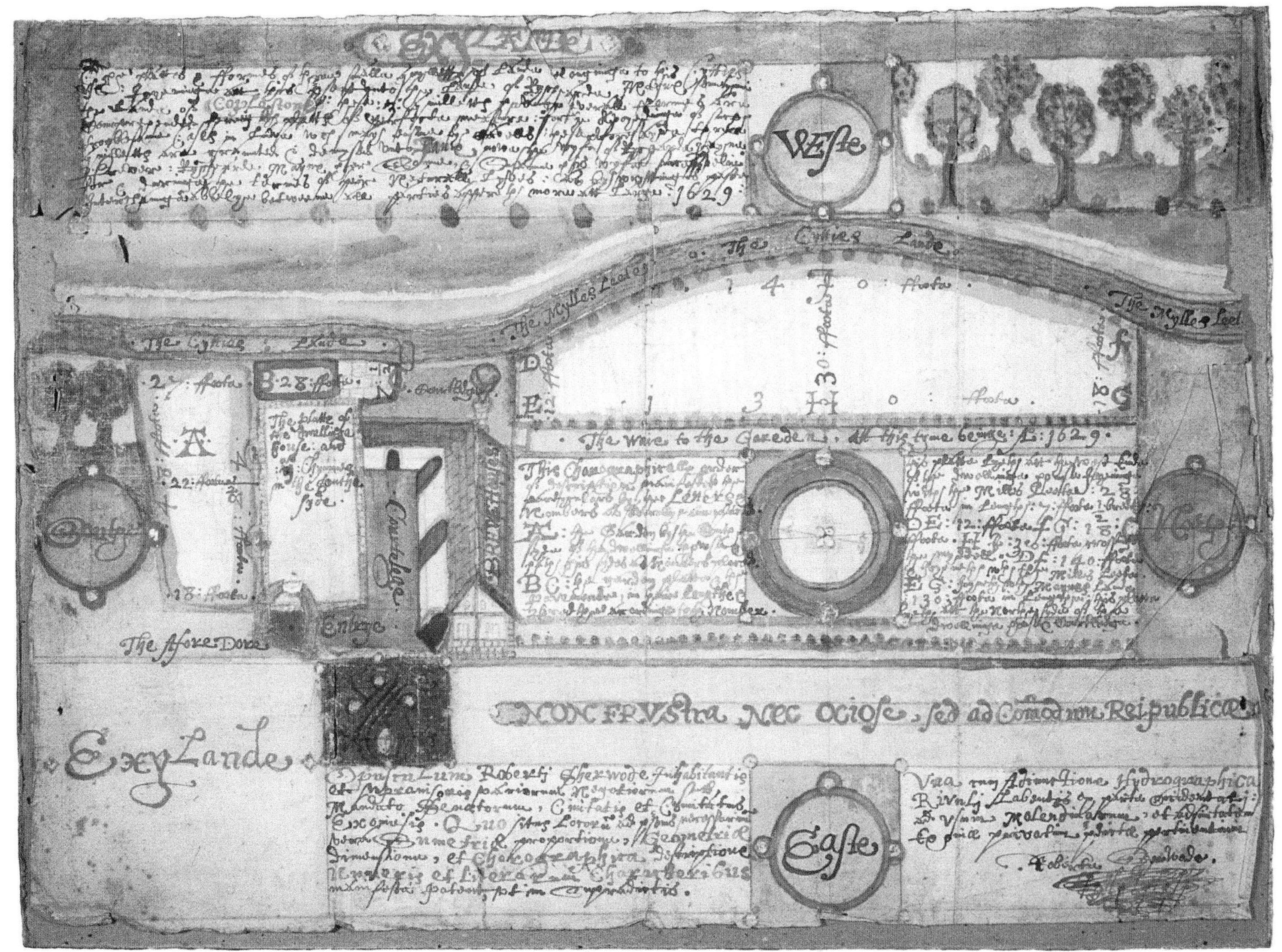
Weste
The Cyties Lande
The Mylles Leete
Easte
Exeylande
NON FRUSTRA NEC OCIOSE, sed ad Comodum Rei publicae

Map 19

꧁ 19 ꧂

Exeter, Exe Island

REFERENCE: Exe Bridge SX 915921
TITLE: 'Exyland'
SURVEYOR: Robert Sherwood ('Sherwode')
SCALE: not given

SIZE: 31.5 cms EW x 44 cms NS
MATERIAL: paper, coloured
ORIENTATION: west to top

DESCRIPTION AND COMMENT

This is the third map of Exe Island drawn by Robert Sherwood and its inset states that it was concerned with 'The plattes & Formes of three small quyllettes of Lande belonginge to this Cytties Use'. These were measured in order to avoid future troublesome cases in law and were granted to Jane, wife of Richard Mayne, and thereafter to her son. The maps are shown with coloured boundaries and with measurements marked between various points distinguished by letters, which are referenced to a second inset panel. Sherwood's letter to the City authorities[1] mentions a garden which can be identified.

At the bottom of the map, on either side of the circle designating east, is a panel of text in Latin in which Sherwood describes his authority from the City of Exeter to draw the map and assures the City of the care and accuracy with which he has carried out his task. In spite of this claim Sherwood does not give any indication of scale on any of his three Exe Island maps and when measurements are related to his figures there is a wide variation of between 16 feet and 23 feet to the inch.

It is interesting to note that the same quillets of land mentioned here are described as being of the heirs of Mayne in a map book of Exeter Chamber lands made *circa* 1756[2] which may be seen on the right.

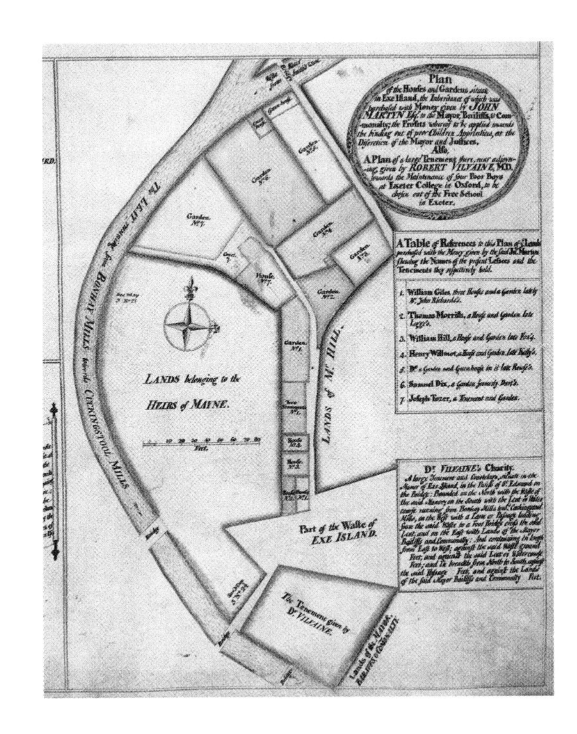

[1] DRO, ECA, Letter 182.
[2] DRO, ECA, Book 58.

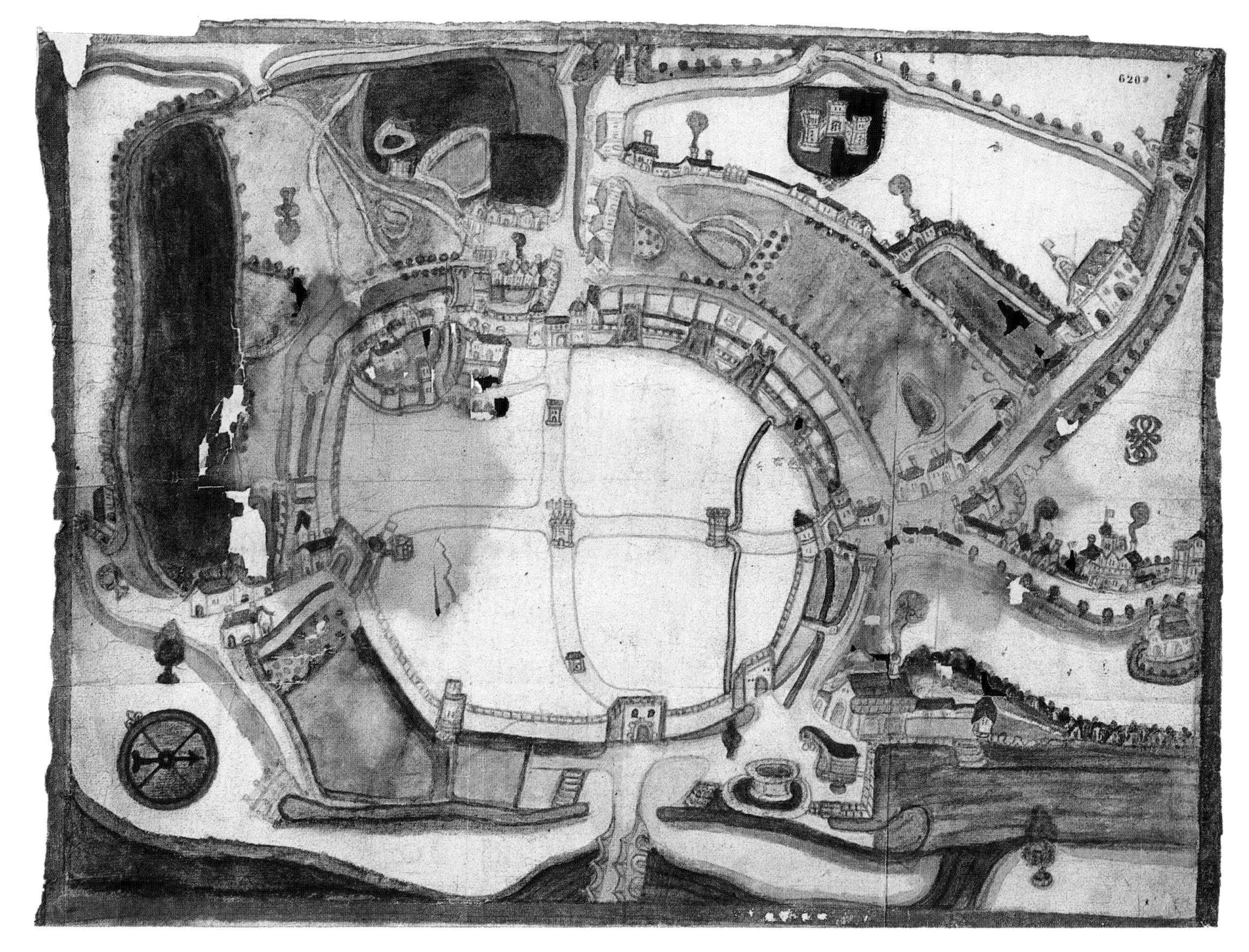

Map 20

20

Exeter, Northernhay and Southernhay

REFERENCE: Exeter East Gate SX 922928
TITLE: not given
SURVEYOR: Robert Sherwood
SCALE: not given
SIZE: 44.7 cms EW x 59.7 cms NS
MATERIAL: paper, coloured
ORIENTATION: north to top left

DESCRIPTION AND COMMENT

This map of the City was drawn by Robert Sherwood at the age of 81 and produced as evidence in a law suit which concerned the ownership of Northernhay and Southernhay in 1632 and 1633 between the City and the Crown.[1] The City walls are shown in some detail as are the defensive towers on the south east quarter and the gates into the City, including the entry into the Cathedral Close.

The Northernhay paths and trees are drawn and coloured. A gate and stile mentioned by Sherwood in his evidence can be distinguished. He stated that about 30 years before, i.e. *circa* 1603, these had been moved away from the North Gate and it is interesting to note that on John Hooker's printed map of 1587 the same gate is placed close to the North Gate of the City. St David's church is shown – the resting place of those whose bodies passed through Northernhay on their way to burial. In Southernhay there are two ponds and tree symbols marking the newly-planted hedge, but it is the small gardens which, in 1575, replaced the 'stinckeing' ditch, and the blue line of the lead pipe taking water from the 'well spring' through the Bishop's Palace gardens to the conduit in South Street which catch the eye. Sherwood has also marked the continuation of this lead pipe to the Watergate and shows water pouring freely below the wall nearby. On the west, in the industrial quarter, there is the mill at Bonhay and the crane on the quay where there are steps to water level.

Sherwood received forty shillings for making this and other maps in June 1633.[2] There is also an undated map of the City in his hand in the City Archives which is not reproduced in this volume. It appears to be based on Hooker's printed map but he has added details of importance to the City in the early seventeenth century. It is probably dated about 1630. Sherwood died in 1640 and the Administration of his will was granted in the Archdeaconry Court of Exeter.

1. DRO, ECA, Law Papers Box 40. Part of Sherwood's Deposition is shown below.
2. DRO, ECA, Act Book VII, 847.

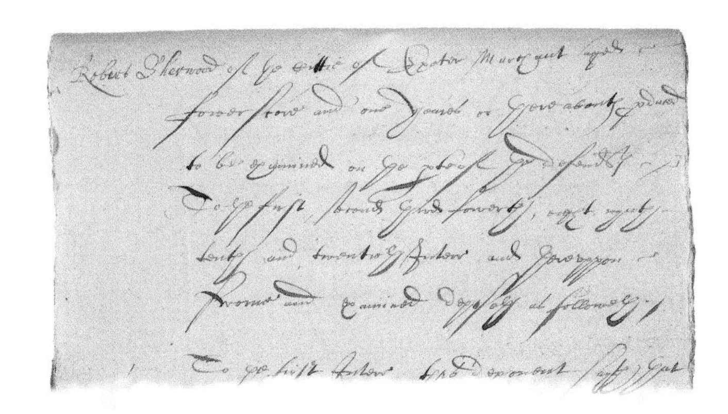

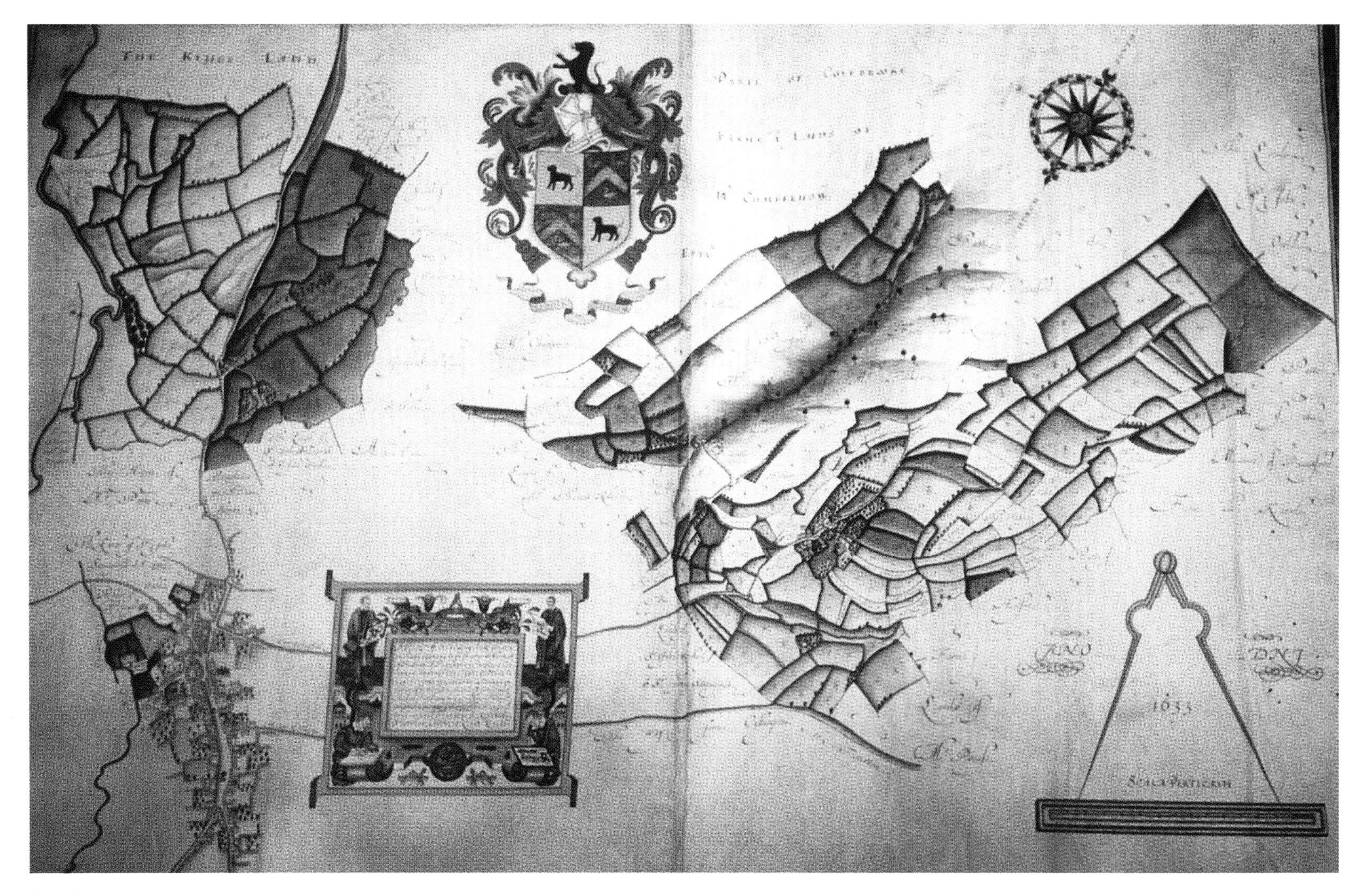

Map 21

21

Cullompton, Padbrook and Ponsford

REFERENCE: Padbrook Hill ST 016060 Ponsford ST 001074 Cullompton ST 022072
TITLE: 'A Plat & Description of all the Landes belonging to the Barton & Mannor of Padbrooke & Paunsford in ye Parishes of Cullumpton & Bradninch in the Countye of Devon'
SURVEYOR: Mark Pierce, also recorded as Pierse

SCALE: 1" = 20 perches; 1:3960
SIZE: 115.5 cms x 76.6 cms
MATERIAL: parchment, coloured
ORIENTATION: south-east to top; 16 point compass rose with 64 divisions in the outer circle

DESCRIPTION AND COMMENT

This handsome map and the accompanying Survey Book were ordered by Sir William Courten of Wingham Barton, Kent and made for him by Mark Pierce, a cartographer also from Kent. The Barton and Manor of Padbrook and Ponsford were probably acquired by Sir William, a wealthy merchant, as an investment, and a map and survey would have been essential preliminaries to profitable estate management and development. The colourful coat of arms and the features incorporated into the title cartouche bear witness to Sir William's importance and his trading interests in the Levant and across the Atlantic. The cartouche is also significant in that the mapmaker can be identified by it even though his name is neither on the map nor in the Survey Book. It shows two illustrations of the surveyor at work writing the Survey and constructing the map with the tools of his craft between; above, the steward or bailiff is using the Survey Book and the map. Identical figures appear on a later map of 1635 which is signed by Mark Pierce; it is of the estate at Laxton in Nottinghamshire also purchased by Sir William Courten. These same four figures appear in the border surrounding the title together with identical fruit and flowers although the later map is decorated additionally with butterflies, ladybirds and snails.

The map, illustrated opposite, which has become known as the Cullompton Map, shows in detail and with great accuracy the fields and farms of Padbrook and Ponsford. Between the two lies the stream rising at Colebrook which supplied Cullompton with water; colour is used to suggest the slopes of the river valley. It is fortunate that Sir William's estate included some land in Cullompton and so the town is also shown. Two buildings in particular attract the eye; the parish church, described by W.G. Hoskins as one of the grandest in Devon, and the house now known as Walronds which was begun in 1603 by Sir John Petre and completed in 1605. Their slate roofs are indicated by blue colour to distinguish them from the other town houses which have red roofs (in this county, possibly thatch). The street pattern can easily be identified on modern maps.

Sir William Courten's connections with Devon seem to have been restricted to this manor and to lands in Crediton. Courten died in 1636, a very wealthy man in spite of considerable losses in newly-opened trade with China and it is probable that these estates were then sold. Unfortunately no documents survive to shed light on what happened to Padbrook and Ponsford after the map was made.

See also:
Mary Ravenhill, 'Sir William Courten and Mark Pierce's Map of Cullompton 1633' in *Devon Documents*, Todd Gray, ed., *DCNQ* Special Issue (1996), xix–xxiii.
A. Sarah Bendall, *Maps, Land and Society* (Cambridge, 1992), 139–40.

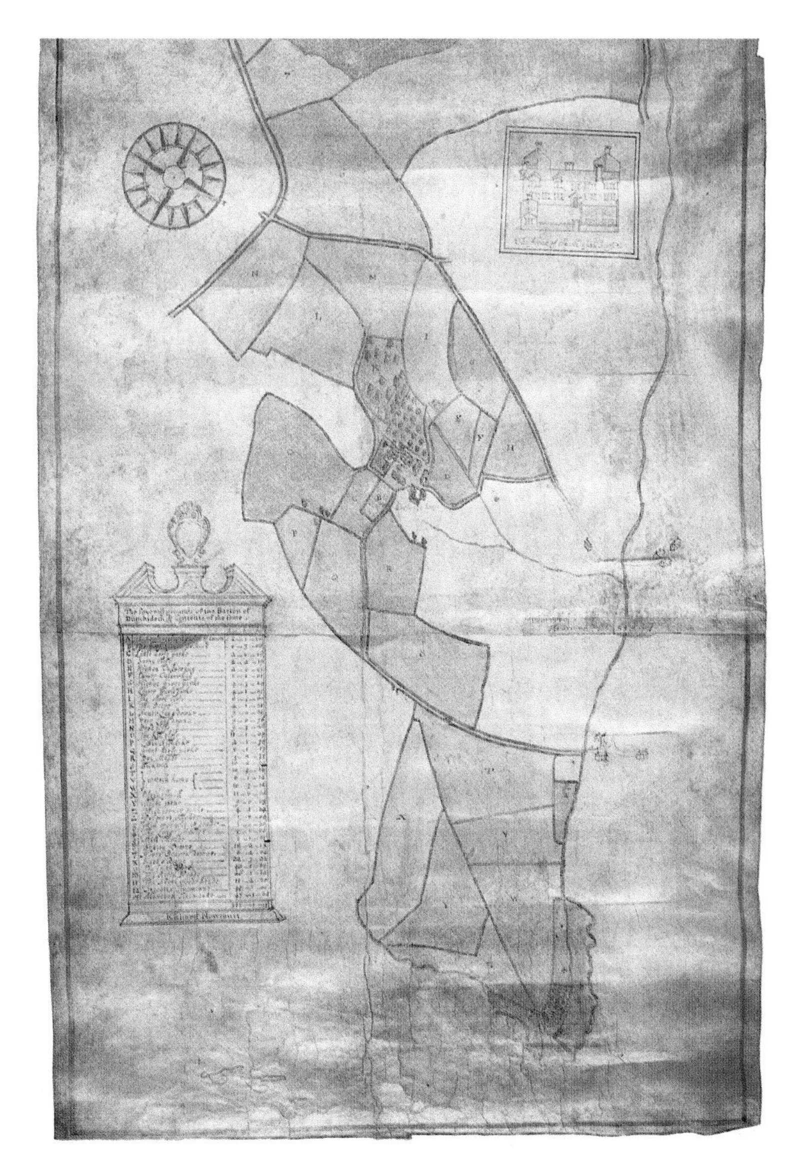

Map 22 – bottom

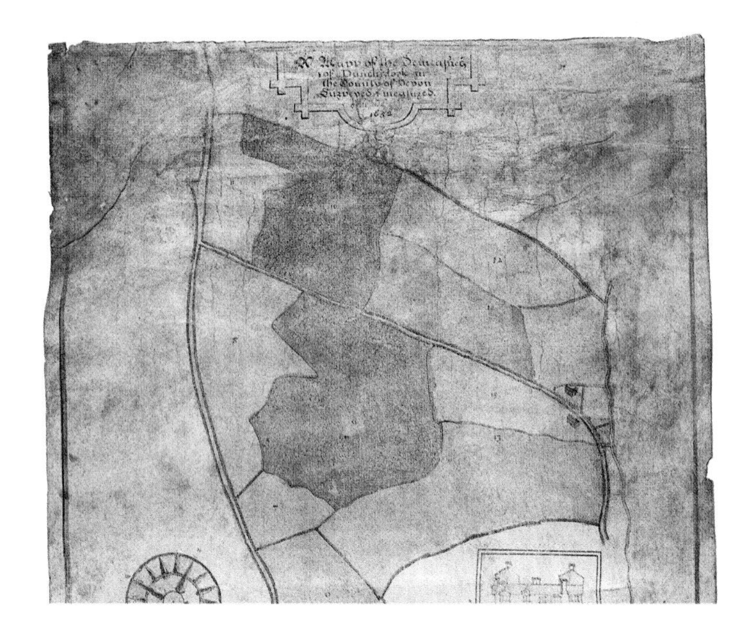

Map 22 – top

꧁ 22 ꧂
Dunchideock

REFERENCE: Dunchideock Church SX 876877
TITLE: 'A Mapp of the Demeasnes of Dunchidock in the County of Devon Surveyed & measured August 1652'
SURVEYOR: Richard Newcourt

SCALE: 'The Decimall Chayne of 4 perch'
SIZE: 50.3 cms EW x 107 cms NS
MATERIAL: parchment, coloured
ORIENTATION: north to top, 16 point compass rose

DESCRIPTION AND COMMENT

Evidently the map was drawn for the Pitman family whose members are listed in the parish in the 1641 Protestation Returns and in the 1674 Hearth Tax Returns. It covers the several grounds of the Barton of Dunchideock and shows the river, bridges, hedges round fields, gates, lanes and houses and the church in elevation. The reference table, in a plain frame with a pediment surmounted by a shield, gives the names of the fields and their acreage. The Pitman family still owned the farm at the time of the making of the tithe map, *circa* 1840. It is assumed that the 'Mansion House' which is shown as an inset view is a representation of the farmhouse rather than of Dunchideock House which was later owned by the Walronds, as no property is shown on the side of the river where Dunchideock House stands.

The advantage of including a view of the principal house on a map was advocated by William Leybourn in his book *The Complete Surveyor* first published in 1653. He states 'Also in your Plot must be expressed the Manor House according to its symmetry or situation, with all other Houses of note, also all water-mils, wind-mils, and whatsoever else is necessary, that may be put into your Plot without confusion'.

Details such as the scale and the compass rose point to a professional surveyor and although this is the earliest recorded work of Richard Newcourt, he went on to produce maps of London in 1658 and was described as a 'topographical draughtsman'. He came from a gentry family which originated in North Devon but his father, Philip, held land in Tiverton. Richard was baptised at Tiverton on 5 August 1599. A connection between Richard Newcourt and the Pitman family has not been established, nor has the reason for making the map.

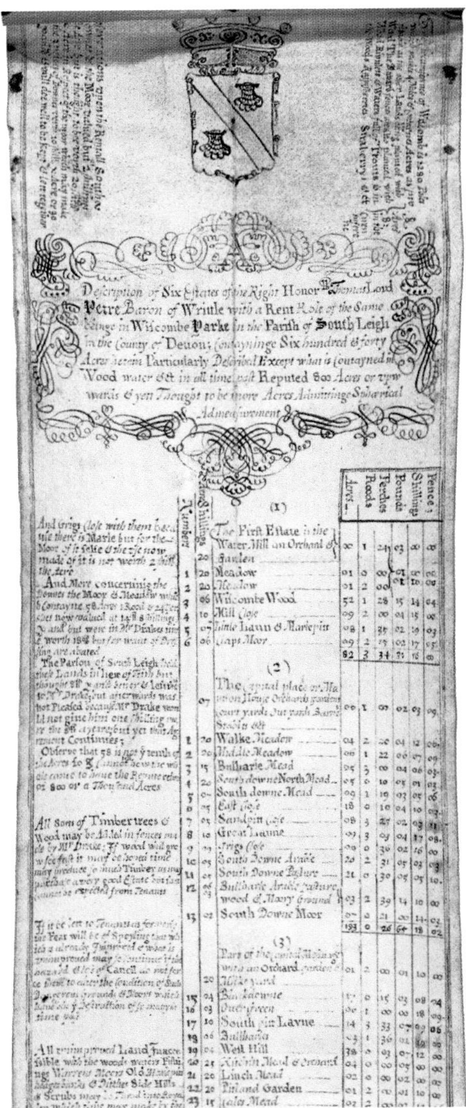

Map 23 – top

Kitchin Mead & Orchard
Linch Mead
Pitland Garden
(4)
Newhouse Close
North Pitt Lawne
Woodcocks Pitt
Part of North Downe West
Part of North Downe East
North Downe
(5)
White Moor Mead
Part of Homminge Quarter
Part of Homminge Quarter
Part of Homminge Quarter
Part of Homminge Quarter
The Old Court & Marle pitt
6
In the Warren Hill
Whitemor Mead
·Wee·
Whose Names are hereunto Subscribed have made A Rent Role & yearly value of these Barts
Sam: Clode : Sam Clode Junr
Broad Downe
Horne Downe
West Hill
Bull Harie
South Downe
Wiscombe Wood
Burrow Land
Castle Downe
Southleigh Common
Blackberry Castle
The full number of Acres in Wiscombe Parke are found to be 637
Kilmington
Axminster
Shute
Drake
Colliton
Wiscombe Parke
Southleigh
Branscom
Sidmouth
Axmouth

Map 23 – bottom

23

Southleigh, Wiscombe Park

REFERENCE: Wiscombe Park SY 187931

TITLE: 'A Description of Six Estates of the Right Honorlb Thomas Lord Petre Baron of Writtle with a Rent Role of the Same beinge in Wiscomb Park in the Parish of South Leigh in the County of Devon; Contayning Six hundred & forty Acres therein Particularly described Except what is Contayned in Wood water &ct in all time past Reputed 800 Acres or upwards & yett Thought to be more Acres Admitting Sphaerical Admeasurement'

SURVEYORS: 'Wee whose Names are hereunto Subscribed have made A Rent Role and year[l]y valueof the whole Particulars to the best of our Knowledge with Moderation &c Consideration to Quantitie & Quallitie by which it may bee seen how this Estate hath bin Improved & what may hereafter appear to Posteritie in what lyeth yet unimproved Samuel Clode Samuel Clode junior Thomas Cookney and John Coffyn'[1]

SCALE: 'The Scale of Perches';1" = 120 perches; 1:23,760 and 'The Scale of Miles';1" = 4 miles; 1:253,440

SIZE: 15.5 cms EW x 73.3 cms NS

MATERIAL: parchment on original small wooden roller, coloured

ORIENTATION: north to top; 16 point compass rose

DESCRIPTION AND COMMENT

This map shows part of the estate of Thomas Lord Petre, Baron of Writtle. Although usually associated with Essex the Petre family also possessed estates in east Devon, Wiscombe Park having been acquired by Sir William Petre in 1574. The map, though small, contains a wealth of information out of all proportion to its size. The statement by the authors establishes that it was concerned with land management and the means by which the estate had been improved in the past and the possibilities for its development in the future. Marginal notes beside the Reference Table elaborate this theme in some detail, enumerating not only the shortcomings of some tenants which have led to a reduction in land values but also the ways in which such failures could be rectified.

A second map, on a smaller scale, shows the position of Wiscombe Park in relation to the principal settlements in east Devon. This extends from 'Lime' in the east to 'Withicomb' and 'Excester' in the west; to the north there are the towns of 'Hunnington' and Chard and in the south 'Pars Maris Britannici'. The symbols used to indicate the towns are reminiscent of Saxton's style – red spots surrounded by a three-towered symbol – and it is possible that Saxton's map of Devonshire was the basis of this small-scale map.

Decorative features add much to the map; the title cartouche with its coat of arms above, the elaborate compass rose where we are told of 'Marle pits how they may be Improved by planting Timber Trees'. The coat of arms has on each side, information about the circumference of the estate, its valuation and the smaller, rather charming details, that 'The Inward Fences are also planted with Wood Rivulets of Waters full of Trouts & in the Woods Raspisberries Straberrys'. The fourth-century B.C. hill fort of Blackberry Castle is named and framed in black by a simple scroll design.

1. The authors of this map were no doubt estate employees for their names appear on no other maps. An account of Samuel Clode's for 1705–6 includes a payment to him for drawing the rental and assisting the Reeve (DRO, 123M/E611). The Bishop's Transcripts for the second half of the seventeenth century include the names *Clode* and *Cookney* which point to Samuel Clode and Thomas Cookney being local men: *DRO, Early Bishop's Transcripts, Southleigh, Reel 32.*

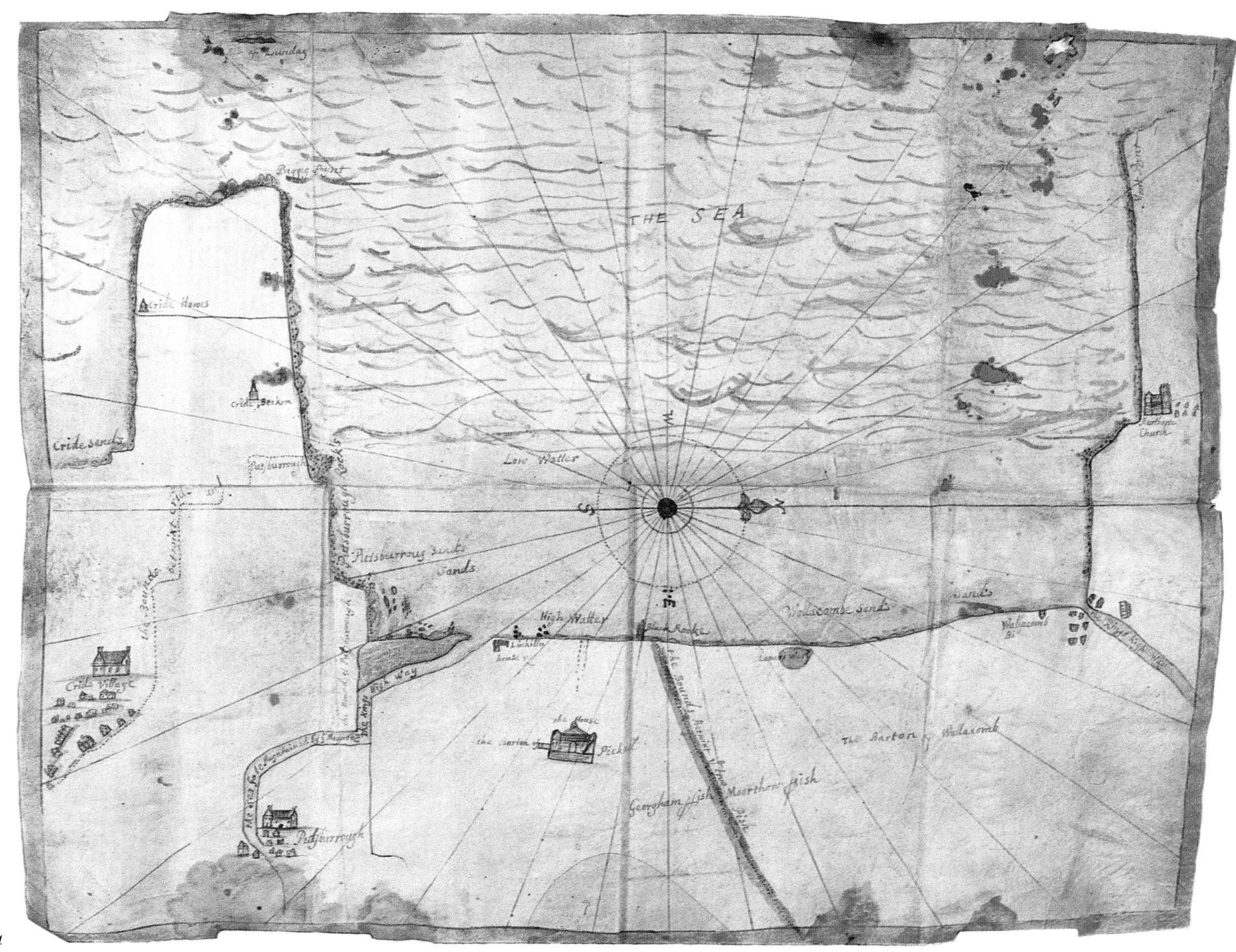
THE SEA
Low Watter
High Watter
Cride Village
Cride Beckon
Sands
Wollacomb Sands
Pitsburrough
The Barton of Wollacomb
Georgham Pish
Moorthow Pish

Map 24

℘ 24 ℘

Georgeham and Mortehoe, Croyde and Putsborough

REFERENCE: Georgeham SS 465399; Putsborough SS 449402
TITLE: not given
SURVEYOR: not named [possibly Mr Cornish]
SCALE: not given

SIZE: 44.1 cms EW x 59.7 cms NS
MATERIAL: parchment, coloured
ORIENTATION: west to top, 32 point compass rose

DESCRIPTION AND COMMENT

This is one of a set of three maps in the North Devon Record Office amongst the archives of the Incledon-Webber family, all of which appear to be of similar date and coverage, showing the area from Putsborough Sands to Woolacombe and Croyde Sands. The map illustrated here marks the sea by green wave lines and high and low water marks are shown. Cliffs and off-shore rocks and the 'Isle of Lunday' are indicated as is the 'Sea Gate mayntained by ye Mannor'. Buildings shown in elevation include Pickwell House and 'Cride village', 'Putsburrough', 'Moorthowe Church', 'Linkilln House' on the shore and 'Cride Beakon' may also be seen.

The maps were evidently drawn up to support a law suit. The lands of Mr Webber, plaintiff, are shown on one of the maps.[1] There are also papers relating to a case between Mr Lewes Incledon against John Harris, William Lewes, John Austyn, William Nutt, Peter Parminter, Humphrey Tallin and Anthony Philp concerning the removal of brandy casks and other items claimed as wreck by Incledon[2] which may well be connected. In these papers is an account dated 12 September 1690 of Henry Jones to Captain Incledon which includes an item 'pd Cornish for culloringe the Mapp 1s' and also an undated account for the new drawing of a map for 2s.6d.

1. NDRO, 3704M/E2/3.
2. NDRO, 3704M/LL8.

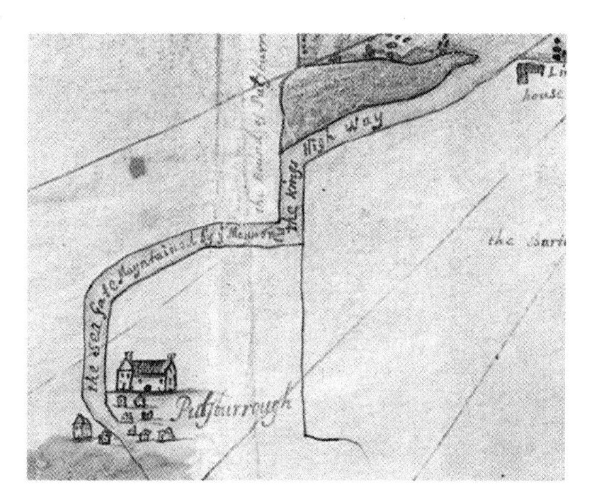

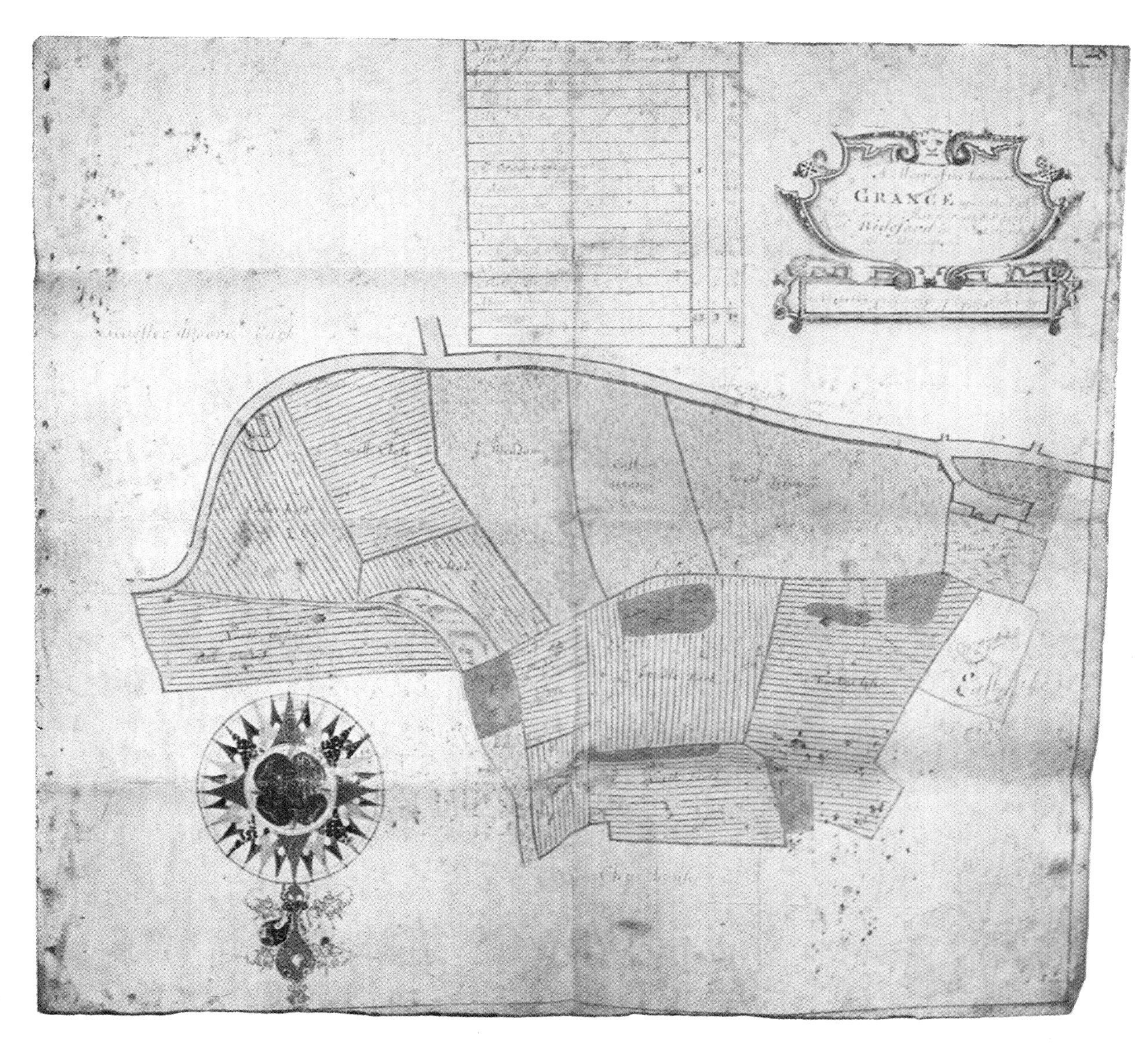

Map 25

25

Bideford, Grange, East-the-Water

REFERENCE: East-the-Water SS 465264
TITLE: 'A Mapp of the Tenement of Grange upon the East land in the Mannor and Parish of Bideford in the County of Devon'
SURVEYOR: Joel Gascoyne

SCALE: 'A Scale of Perches'; 1" = 10 perches; 1:1980
SIZE: 46.4 cms EW x 42.4 cms NS
MATERIAL: parchment, coloured
ORIENTATION: south to top; 32 point compass rose

DESCRIPTION AND COMMENT

This map of lands in the tenement of Grange in the manor and parish of Bideford can with some confidence be attributed to Joel Gascoyne.

After a career in London as a chartmaker Gascoyne turned to land surveying.[1] He came to the South West some time after 1693 and surveyed some 258 landholdings for Baron Robartes of Lanhydrock between 1694 and 1699. At the same time he surveyed and produced, in 1699, his near one-inch-to-the-mile map of Cornwall. Gascoyne had also produced an Atlas of some 33 estate maps for the Grenville family of Stowe near Kilkhampton and so the move to map the Grenville lands in the Manor of Bideford could be a logical progression. The inclusion of the number 28 on the top right corner of the map and the suggestion of stitching on the left side implies that the map of Grange was part of another Atlas.

The map shows fields north of the road from Bideford. Green is used to colour these fields but even so their use is clearly differentiated. Arable land has brown lines superimposed on the green background; green fields stippled with a deeper green are also classed as arable but this may well indicate those which were meadow/fallow at the time of mapping. Other areas in a pale green with darker shading are described as moor. Wood and orchard are shown with tree symbols. A table lists the field names, their 'Qualleties' (i.e. land use) and 'Quanteties' and this, with the colour and symbols seen here, is typical of all Gascoyne's work which was designed to provide the information required for effective estate management. In addition, the design and colour used in the cartouche and compass rose are characteristic and enable correct attribution to be made of many unsigned maps. Included among these are two maps in the Devon Record Office, unfinished and without title and as yet unidentified, but without doubt by Gascoyne's hand.[2]

Following the completion of his map of Cornwall, Gascoyne published Proposals for a similar map of Devon.[3] It is reasonable to suggest that maps of Devon estates would have formed the basis for such a county map; the Grenville landholdings would have been a suitable starting point, and this map of Grange could well have been one of them. But it was not to be for the death in 1701 of John Grenville, Earl of Bath, deprived Gascoyne of his patron and no doubt led to the failure of the project. It is Devon's loss that Joel Gascoyne did not produce a map of the county similar to his map of Cornwall. The latter, the first near one-inch-to-the-mile county map represented a significant, and at the time unique, advance in large-scale county mapping.

1. William Ravenhill, 'Joel Gascoyne a Pioneer of Large-Scale County Mapping', *Imago Mundi* XXVI (1972), 60–70.
2. DRO, 1948 Pearse/Maps.
3. BL, Bagford Collection, Harl. MS. 5496 f.78, reproduced in *Imago Mundi* XXVI (1972), 67.

The compass rose illustrated on the inside front cover of this volume is to be found in the Atlas of the Grenville estates near Kilkhampton, known as the Stowe Atlas. This is now in the Cornwall Record Office, DD X 273. It shows quite clearly that the map opposite was the work of the same cartographer.

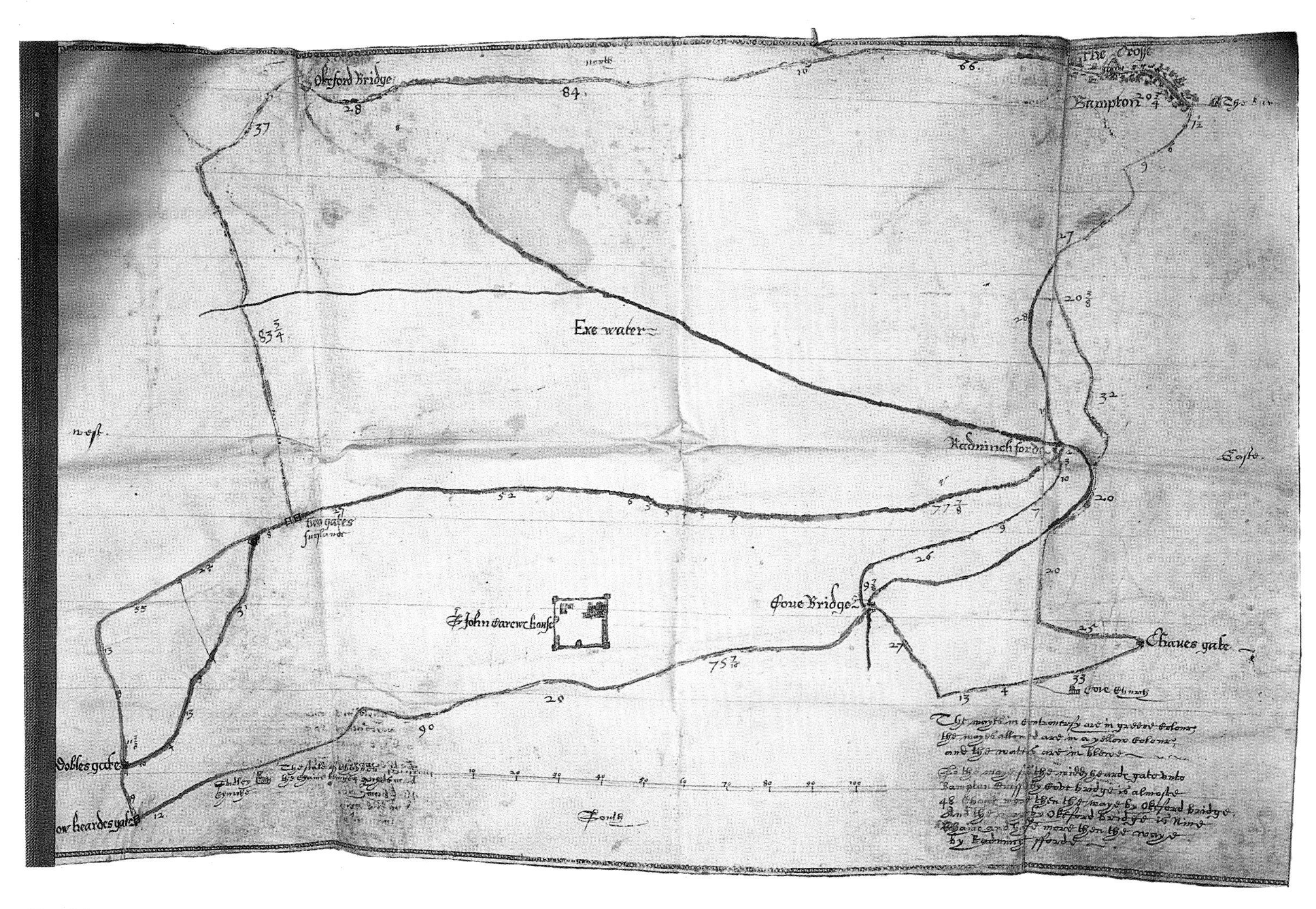

Okeford Bridge
The Crosse
Bampton
Exe water
west
Easte
Two gates
Cove Bridge
Cove Church
South

Map 26

26

Stoodleigh

REFERENCE: SS 936197
TITLE: not given
SURVEYOR: not named
SCALE: 'The Scale of Chaynes the Chaine beinge 4 perches'; 1" = 13 chains; 1:10,296; 'The Scale of feete'; 1" = 12 feet; 1:144

SIZE: 67cms EW x 38.3cms NS
MATERIAL: parchment, slight colour
ORIENTATION: north to top; directions spelt out on margins

DESCRIPTION AND COMMENT

The map of Stoodleigh (opposite) and the accompanying house plan (see p. 58) present more problems than might at first appear when attempting to assign a date. Sir John Carew's will, dated 14 October 1636 and proved 1 May 1637, makes it clear that he was concerned with the maintenance of Carew Castle in Pembrokeshire and in building 'Mansion' houses at his manors of Camerton in Somerset and East Stoodleigh in Devon. Sir John did not achieve his ambitions in his lifetime for on his death his will directed that 'my son (his heir) Thomas Carew shall build a Mansion House at Studleigh in Devon. My son John Carew shall build a Mansion House at Camerton. My son George Carew shall reeidify Carew Castle with four towers, covered with lead...'[1] There is no evidence that either Thomas or John carried out their father's wishes. As far as Thomas was concerned no doubt the fine imposed by Parliament in August 1646 of £1085 for his delinquency, in addition to the money he had collected 'for Maintenance of the Forces raised against Parliament'[2] inhibited his house-building activities.

The evidence provided by the map and the house plan shows that neither was made for Thomas Carew. The house outlined on the map opposite is clearly identified as 'Sir John Carewe's House' and equally clearly represents a simplified outline of the more detailed 'mappe of a house to be builded at East Studley'; the word 'southe' seems identical on map and plan and would suggest that both are by the same hand and thus probably are of the same date, which would be prior to Sir John Carew's death in 1637.

The map is concerned with a comparison of distances between 'widd[ow] heardes gate' and Bampton Cross comparing three routes, one by way of Oakford Bridge, a second by Cove Bridge and the third by 'Radninch Forde'. The legend states that 'The wayes in Controversy are in a greene Colour, the wayes allowed are in a yellow Colour, and the waters are in blewe'; but unfortunately this distinction is no longer clear for the colours have deteriorated with the passage of time. This loss of clarity in the blue, yellow and green colours is indicative of the nature of the pigments in use in the seventeenth century. Blue, most probably indigo, used for Exe Water has altered least but the yellow and green are difficult to distinguish one from the other. Saffron yellow and a yellow called masticot were the shades recommended at this time while the green used was most probably that known as verdigris. Even seventeenth-century writers warned of its lack of durability and incompatibility with other pigments.

The ground plan of Sir John Carew's house on the map, although substantially the same as the 'architect's' drawing, does show some differences. An entrance on the west and structures within the internal courtyard are not present in the plan on the following page. The latter is interesting in many ways; it has castle-like features in the arrangement of the inner courtyard with its four corner towers but the introduction of living rooms within those towers and beside the connecting walls reflects changes found in late sixteenth and early seventeenth-century houses. Thus the hall with the buttery and kitchen close by, the parlour and lodging chambers together with the dairy and store house are all to be found on the ground floor.

The first floor (described as the 'seconde storie') repeats this arrangement of rooms but unfortunately their use is not indicated. It is interesting to note that the centrally-placed hall door presents a symmetrical facade, that windows are many but that no doorways, other than those between the hall and kitchen and buttery, are evident. It was the practice for entry to other rooms to be made from the courtyard but that would leave the lodging chamber in the north-west tower and the dairy without means of entry – an interesting problem compounded on the first floor. Sir John's 'architect' was leaving much to the builders.

Attempts to identify any evidence of the existence of Sir John Carew's house have proved disappointing. The Tithe Map shows an intriguing square enclosure merely labelled 'garden'. The building close by at East Stoodleigh Barton is listed Grade II; parts date from the seventeenth century and lie alongside one side of the garden. It is possible that part of the wall of Sir John Carew's property could have been incorporated into this building.

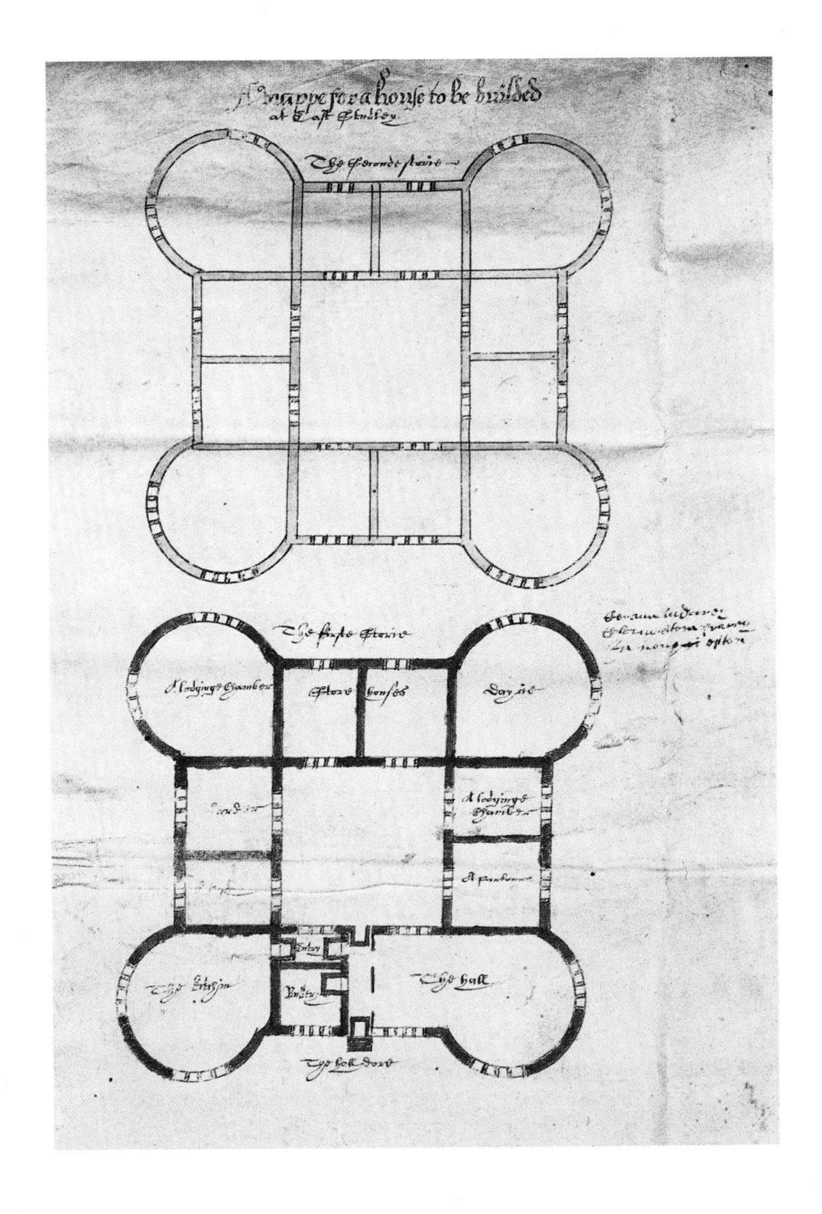

[1] F.A. Crisp, *Abstracts of Somersetshire Wills Third Series* (Privately printed, 1889), 25.
[2] *House of Commons Journals*, (1644–1646), 635–6.

See also:

Bridget Cherry, 'The Devon Country House in the Late Seventeenth and Early Eighteenth Centuries', *Devon Archaeological Society Proceedings* 46 (1988), 91–137.